D1537373

Dear Brides- and Grooms-to-Be,

I'm delighted you've chosen this book to help you plan your special day. Your wedding should be everything you've dreamed and hoped for, and good planning—relying on not only yourselves but your cherished loved ones—makes it happen.

I've updated this guide to include special lists for the bride and groom, made up of tips from recently married men and women from across the country, sharing wisdom and ideas they wish they'd had when they were planning *their* big day. I hope you'll enjoy their suggestions, and that after you've walked down the aisle yourself, you'll share what you've learned as well.

Remember, a special wedding requires forethought and consideration, but it also comes from the heart. Don't let the hectic months and weeks leading up to your big day whip you into a panic; don't forget the people in your life who are helping you plan and carry off the festivities; don't let little spills and glitches (and there are bound to be a few) blind you to the overall beauty and meaning of the occasion; and most of all, don't forget to share the emotions and excitement of the experience with your beloved wedding partner, who will walk with you not just down the aisle, but down the path of your life together. Remember to be kind, to be loving, and to be prepared.

Wishing you a lifetime of happiness,

Marjabelle Young Stewart

THE COMPLETE WEDDING PLANNER

Also by Marjabelle Young Stewart

Commonsense Etiquette
The New Etiquette
Little Ways to Say I Love You
Executive Etiquette in the New Workplace (with Marian Faux)
Complete Book of Modern Table Manners

Written with Ann Buchwald
White Gloves and Party Manners
Stand Up, Shake Hands, Say "How Do You Do"
What to Do When—and Why

THE COMPLETE WEDDING PLANNER

The Essential Guide to Planning
Every Phase of Your Wedding

Second Revised Edition

Marjabelle Young Stewart

Illustrations by Diana Thewlis

ST. MARTIN'S GRIFFIN

N E W   Y O R K

THE COMPLETE WEDDING PLANNER. Copyright © 2002, 1989 by Marjabelle Young Stewart. Illustrations copyright © 1989 by Diana Thewlis. All rights reserved. Printed in the United States of America. No part of this book may be used or reproduced in any manner whatsoever without written permission except in the case of brief quotations embodied in critical articles or reviews. For information, address St. Martin's Press, 175 Fifth Avenue, New York, N.Y. 10010.

Design by Glen M. Edelstein

www.stmartins.com

Library of Congress Cataloging-in-Publication Data

Stewart, Marjabelle Young.
    The Complete Wedding Planner
    Second rev. ed. of: Your complete wedding planner
        p. cm.
    ISBN 0-312-27711-3
    1. Wedding etiquette.   I. Stewart, Marjabelle Young. Your Complete Wedding Planner.   II. Title.

BJ2051.S73   1989
395'.22   88–29905

ISBN 0-312-27711-3

First published in the United States by St. Martin's Griffin under the title *Your Complete Wedding Planner*

Second Revised Edition: April 2002

10 9 8 7 6 5 4 3 2 1

To Erin and Shannon,
Jackie and John,
Sherri and Bill,
with love, laughter,
and happy ever after.

CONTENTS

ACKNOWLEDGMENTS

My special thanks go to the following for their help: Marian Faux, for her superb literary skills and invaluable help in producing this book; Barbara Anderson, my editor, Anne Savarese, Joy Chang, Ingrid Ducmanis, and the Reverend Craig B. Chapman for their professional know-how and fine attention to detail; Dominick Abel, my agent, for his years of beautiful friendship and true caring in guiding my career; Maxine Johnson, Eleanore Osterkamp, Dorothy Carow Merrick, Patt McIntyre, Sue Barnes, Elaine Cokinos, Mary Workman, Jerelyn Packee, Carol McReynolds, Rosemary Paxton, Eva Stuenkel, Ellene Paulsen, Margaret Rankin, Irene Caruso, Shirley Neill, Linda Gardner, Katherine Mursener, Donna Bensenberg, and Marion Murphy for their research, diplomacy, brilliance, and endless humor; Diana Thewlis, for the drawings in the book; and to the over 100,000 beautiful brides who have used this book and made it a bestseller.

INTRODUCTION

Your wedding day is perhaps *the* most special day of your life. Even though you will enjoy other special occasions, few will compare with the beauty and love in which you will be showered on your wedding day. A wedding is both a moment of great privacy and intimacy and a public and ceremonial event. For some people, it is also a major production of theatrical proportions. Regardless of the kind of wedding you have, though, whether it is elaborate or simple, large or small, it will require a lot of thought, planning, and loving attention to detail.

This book is designed to help you have the wedding of your dreams. It guides you through every phase of your wedding—choosing your attendants, selecting a caterer, planning the flowers—and the events that surround it, including the engagement party, showers, rehearsal dinner, reception, and honeymoon.

You will also discover many ways to add personal touches that will make your wedding unique, as well as advice about planning a wedding that is both tasteful and fun. I'll cover the smallest details, such as the preparation of rice packages for your guests to throw at you as you leave the church, and the more important aspects of getting married, such as how to arrange your life so it can be shared with another person. Included at the back of this book is a special Bride's Organizer, a section designed to help you handle all the details (and there will be more than you ever imagined!) of your wedding. Also included is a Household Organizer to help you plan your new home.

This book is geared to helping you plan a wedding that suits you and that is in keeping with the times. Fashion in weddings, like much else in life, tends to be cyclical. In the 1960s, weddings were more casual. Couples got married anywhere but in a church or temple—on hills, at beaches, in parks. They often wore unusual clothes—anything but the traditional white dress and black or white tie. Barefoot weddings were in, and formal ones were out. Many of the old rules of etiquette were thrown out, and some new rules had to be invented to cover new situations. We learned that second-time-around and older brides could look lovely in white, that some wedding dresses looked better without gloves, and that cohabiting couples could have a traditional wedding. We figured out how to handle new kinds of families—divorced parents, stepparents, step- and half-siblings. With so many people marrying at a late age, couples began to plan and pay for their own weddings.

Today the pendulum has swung back toward formal, traditional weddings, perhaps because we learned that by being too casual about weddings, we diminished their meaning. We dropped the stuffy formality, but we also lost a lot of lovely traditions and customs, which, as we learned with hindsight, matter a great deal. Brides are once again wearing traditional long white dresses and veils, and are being married in the sanctuary of their own church or synagogue. They want their attendants in elegant, lovely clothes. They want lovely flowers and good food and a beautiful cake.

While I'm pleased to see this return to tradition, I do think the Flower Children left us with two worthwhile legacies: a more creative approach to weddings and an emphasis on feelings rather than on ritual. Today's bride can have just about any kind of wedding she wants, but she also is considerate of the feelings of others. Never are rules more important than people's feelings. That's why, in this book, you will find some rules of etiquette, but more often you will find solutions to the situations and problems that inevitably arise whenever a wedding is planned.

Above all, this book is intended to help you, the lovely bride, have the wedding you long for. You will learn how to make everything, right down to the last tiny detail, go smoothly. Good luck—and don't forget to enjoy yourself and your special moment.

THE
COMPLETE
WEDDING
PLANNER

1
A Beginning

WHEN you were a young girl, you probably envisioned your wedding as a chapter in a glowing, golden, fairy tale—glamorous and lovely in every respect—the ultimate happy ending. It can be all that, but arranging a wedding is not always as painless and carefree in reality as it is in your fantasies. And it's not an ending, either. A wedding is a beginning—one that takes a surprising amount of time and energy, and one from which you will want to emerge with an unscathed relationship with your new husband, your family and friends, and his family and friends.

Planning a wedding—even a small one—is a major undertaking, something that requires far more organization than anyone ever imagines. And even though planning a wedding could be a full-time job, today most women work full-time and plan their weddings in their spare time. Then, too, weddings, even the smallest ones, have a way of getting out of hand. Small, intimate gatherings have a way of turning into large, unwanted displays of opulence, and large, formal weddings can be reduced to tense, unhappy occasions.

The first glimmer of reality regarding your wedding will probably set in when you discover that the wedding of your dreams may not be the one your mother has been dreaming of for you. You want flowers that look Victorian, and your mother thinks dried pale pink flowers are just awful. You have found a great wedding dress that just happens to be backless—and your mother is shocked.

You will also find that time is in far shorter supply than you ever imagined, especially in the last weeks before your wedding. You always thought you would spend hours planning the music for your ceremony, but you cannot seem to find the time even to listen to the music you might like to choose.

And throughout it all there will be the relationships. Your wedding day may indeed bring out the best in everyone, but the weeks prior to the wedding often bring out the worst in people. You want to keep the wedding small, for example, but *his* mother is calling you every other day with someone new to add to the guest list, and you don't know how to tell her no tactfully. Your sister, always cooperative until now, insists she cannot wear the shade of blue you have selected for the attendants.

What can you do? How can you handle it all? Easily, if you know what is possible. You need to know what you want and how to get it, how to organize yourself and others, how to plan for every contingency, and above all how to handle everyone with love and tact. In the pages that follow, you will find advice and suggestions on all this.

And now it's time to get started. You've just gotten engaged and, well, what do you do now? What's expected of you? How do you break the good news? Read on and find out.

2
Your Engagement

BREAKING THE NEWS

THE first people to learn your wonderful news should be both sets of parents. Since many couples live in communities far from their parents, they may not have even met this person whom you have decided to marry. If so, try to plan a trip home for the two of you when you break the news. This way, your parents can begin to get acquainted with your fiancé.

Close relatives and friends should be the next to hear about your engagement. Call or write them, whichever suits you, but in any event, those close to you should hear the news from you personally, not by word-of-mouth or reading a newspaper announcement.

As soon as your parents have been told of your plans to marry, they should begin to get acquainted. It is customary for the groom's parents to call on the bride's family, but no one should stand on ceremony. If his mother does not call your mother, encourage your mother to get in touch with his parents. If they live near enough, they should meet over dinner or drinks. If this is not possible, letters expressing everyone's delight over the match should be exchanged. Often when the parents do not know each other because they live in different places, the groom's parents plan to arrive a few days ahead of the wedding so everyone can get acquainted.

THE RINGS

Although many things have changed in our society, so far only the bride wears an engagement ring. Traditionally, it is a gift from the groom-to-be to his betrothed, but the days when a man surprises his beloved by presenting her with a small black velvet box containing a sparkling diamond ring are no longer. Most women, in fact, prefer to be consulted about their engagement ring and some even want to participate actively in its selection. After all, this is a piece of jewelry that you expect to wear every day for the rest of your life. Sometimes the price of the ring is also a joint decision, particularly if a couple is saving for a house or some other major purchase.

However involved you are in the decision about the engagement ring, your funds will rarely be used to buy it. (And in the event the wedding is called off, you are obligated to return the engagement ring and any other pieces of expensive or heirloom jewelry you have been given.)

If the price is a concern, your fiancé can pay the jeweler a visit before he brings you in to try on rings. He can preselect some rings in his price range, which will be shown to you when you come in together.

One woman I know recently developed a new twist on this method of selecting an engagement ring. She loved and knew a lot about antique jewelry and very much wanted an antique engagement ring. Her fiancé knew nothing about antique jewelry—and had little patience for shopping. They settled on a price range and agreed that she would go make the preselection, after which she would bring him in so they could make the final choice together.

Although the diamond has been the engagement stone of preference for several decades now, any stone is appropriate. Diamonds, particularly investment quality ones, are very expensive, and there are many other beautiful precious and semiprecious stones from which to choose. Some stones, such as rubies and emeralds, are more expensive than diamonds, but many others—sapphires, opals, pearls, garnets—are less expensive and make lovely engagement rings. Many women like to wear their birthstones. A chart showing these follows.

January	Garnet
February	Amethyst
March	Aquamarine
April	Diamond
May	Emerald
June	Pearl, Moonstone, or Alexandrite
July	Ruby
August	Sardonyx or Peridot
September	Sapphire
October	Opal or Tourmaline
November	Topaz
December	Turquoise or Zircon

In choosing any kind of stone, it is a good idea to learn a little bit about fine jewelry before you shop, particularly if you will be shopping for a diamond or other precious stone.

Jewelers advise that you know something about the four Cs—clarity, color, cut, and carat—before you shop for precious stones. Clarity refers to the absence of any serious flaws that can be seen not by the naked eye but when the stone is magnified. Color refers to the body color of the stone. Diamonds, for example, come in a variety of tints. Cut refers to the shape of the diamond and the skill with which its facets have been carved. The most popular shapes for precious stones are round, oval, marquise, pear, and emerald. Carat refers to the weight of the stone. A stone may be referred to as one-half carat, one carat, one-and-a-half carats, and so on. These four elements combined define the quality of a stone. Always buy the very best stone you can afford, and buy it from a reputable dealer.

Occasionally, you may be offered an heirloom ring from either one

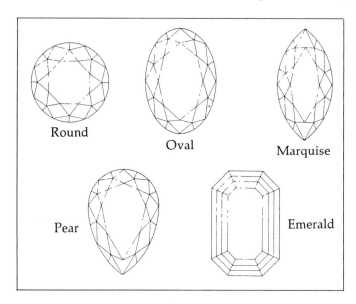

of your families. A genuine antique ring is beautiful, but jewelry that is only one or two generations old has a way of looking merely dated. Either way, if the ring you are offered is not to your taste, you may turn it down tactfully, perhaps by saying you have always wanted a ring that was chosen just for you. Alternately, you might ask whether you can have the stones reset.

When choosing your engagement ring, keep in mind that it will be worn with a wedding band. In fact, many couples buy both rings at the same time, and sometimes, they are part of a matched set. Even if you buy your wedding band later, it's a good idea to try on some wedding rings when you are choosing an engagement ring, to see what looks good together.

The wedding rings are your gifts to each other. Most men wear a ring but some prefer not to—this is, of course, his decision. Matching wedding bands are a sentimental touch, if you can find rings that flatter both your hands. Men's hands are usually larger than women's, and can handle a bigger ring. Keep in mind before choosing a wide band that it can be uncomfortable and sometimes causes skin irritations.

Although the custom is less popular today, it's a lovely idea to have your rings engraved. Your jeweler can do this, or can suggest someone.

The simplest and most frequently used engraving is your initials and the date of your wedding, but you may want to include a short expression of your love: Semper Fidelis (Latin for Always Faithful), Faithfully, Always, Love, or anything else that appeals to you and fits on a small band.

AN ENGAGEMENT PARTY

A party is a festive way to announce your engagement. Close friends and relatives will be aware that an announcement is in the offing, and when they receive an invitation, will not be too surprised. Your parents or other close relatives usually give the engagement party. It may be announced as a party "honoring our daughter and her fiancé, Aaron," or your parents may simply invite everyone to a party. Midway through the party, by way of breaking the news, your father proposes a toast to you and your fiancé. The groom's family and yours and close friends of you and your parents should be invited to the engagement party, which can be as simple or as elaborate as your parents wish.

His parents also may want to give an engagement party to introduce you to their friends and family. And today, when so many couples have established themselves in communities other than their hometowns, you may want to give yourselves a party. When you give the party yourselves, it is more tactful—and fun—not to announce its purpose in advance. This discourages gifts (although people who want to give you an engagement gift will do so anyway) and also lets you announce your good news in any way you choose.

THE FORMAL ANNOUNCEMENT

Formal announcement of an engagement is usually made through a newspaper where you and your fiancé live and in both sets of parents' hometown newspapers. City newspapers today often don't give much space to these announcements. In fact, many newspapers in large cities will announce engagements and weddings only as a paid advertisement. A call to a society page editor will let you know whether or not you should send an announcement. Your parents issue the announcements in their names, although couples who have lived on their own for several years may issue their own announcements.

A few guidelines should be followed in preparing a newspaper announcement. First, if you send a picture of yourself with the announcement, it should be a good 8-x-10-inch glossy print. Second, type the announcement. Do not handwrite it. Each newspaper should be given fresh copy; carbons are not flattering to the society editor who receives them. If you know the name of the society editor, by all means direct the press release to him or her personally. At the top of the announcement, put a release date. The newspaper is bound not to print the notice of your engagement before this date. All newspapers should be given the same release date.

Write the announcement as nearly as possible in the style of the newspaper to which it is submitted. This usually means that the most important information is given first and the less important details follow. Use your and your fiancé's full names; nicknames are not appropriate here. Be sure to give your fiancé's name and address and his parents' names and address.

In addition to the news of your engagement, some newspapers are interested in miscellaneous information about you, such as the following:

- ☐ Your and your fiancé's membership in clubs, fraternities, and sororities
- ☐ Your and your fiancé's business affiliations
- ☐ Your grandparents' names if they are distinguished socially or are prominent in some other way
- ☐ Distinguished ancestors
- ☐ Military service of you or your fiancé
- ☐ Your and your fiancé's fathers' and/or mothers' business affiliations

An announcement should also include the date of the wedding, even if it is as tentative as "A summer wedding is planned."

If you are a minor, your mother's signature may be required on the announcement.

The following form shows the kind of release you can type yourself:

TO: Society Editor   For Release: Sunday, May 1
_____

THE KEWANEE STAR-COURIER

Mr. and Mrs. Donald Park of 522 S. Tremont Street announce the engagement of their daughter, Miss Julia Lea Park, to Mr. Aaron Thomas Jones, son of Mr. and Mrs. Douglas Richard Jones of 333 McClure Street.

Miss Park is a graduate of the University of Chicago. Mr. Jones, a graduate of St. John's Military Academy, is a third-year law student at Harvard University.

If you prefer, you can fill out a copy of the engagement form that follows:

ENGAGEMENT FORM

Please fill out and return to Society Editor.

Full name of bride-elect _____ Phone _____
Residence of bride-elect _____
Parents _____
Parents' residence _____
College and prep schools _____
Social affiliations _____
Family connections _____
Full name of bridegroom-elect _____ Phone _____
Residence of bridegroom-elect _____
Parents _____
Parents' residence _____
College and schools _____
Social affiliations _____
Family connections _____
Date of wedding _____

How engagement is announced _____
Release date _____
Signature of bride-elect or one of her parents
          (Use reverse side for additional information.)

A special place is provided in the Bride's Organizer to keep a copy of your engagement announcement.

3
Wedding Traditions

BEFORE you are caught up in the whirl of activity that inevitably surrounds any wedding, you might want to take a few minutes to consider and perhaps select some of the traditions you want to follow.

Few moments in one's life are as fraught with tradition as one's wedding day. Most wedding customs symbolize the union of two persons. They are intended to reinforce the notion of fertility, constancy, and happiness. Traditions add personal meaning to your wedding and also tie it together symbolically with all other weddings. Some traditions may have been handed down in your family, or you may have observed a custom that particularly appealed to you at another wedding. Or you can choose from among the many traditions described here.

The saying "Happy is the bride the sun shines on" is attributed to the belief held by ancient peoples in the fertilizing power of the sun. In some ancient cultures, the bride was required to rise early on her wedding day and "look into the face of the sun." Sometimes the betrothed couple greeted the sun together, and if the day happened to be a rainy one, the wedding was postponed in favor of a more auspicious time. Today, one naturally hopes a bride will have a sunny wedding day, but weddings are no longer postponed, and there is no record of a rainy day interfering with future happiness—or fertility.

The first wedding tradition you will probably follow is the selection of your rings. The use of rings dates back to the days when a price was paid for a bride. The earliest ones were made of braided grass. Engagement rings first appeared in medieval Italy, but diamond engagement rings did not catch on until a few decades ago, and that was at the prompting of the diamond industry. In many cultures, though, an engagement ring, whether diamond or some other stone, symbolizes the couple's intentions to marry.

The wedding band was initially a bride price, and a plain gold band was required because its value was easily measured. A plain circular wedding band has also symbolized unending love since the days of ancient Egyptians. Early Romans wore iron rings to symbolize the permanent relationship between a husband and wife.

Because ancient peoples believed that the vein in the third finger of the left hand led directly to the heart, wedding rings have traditionally been placed on that finger. The English Book of Prayer in 1549 specified the left hand as appropriate for men and women, and since that time, English-speaking people have worn their rings on their left hands. In some Western European countries, however, the wedding ring is worn on the right hand. Greeks wear their rings on the left hand until they are married and then transfer them to the other hand, and Jews may place the ring on the right hand or the index finger during the ceremony, although most brides later switch it to their left hand, third finger.

The wearing of the wedding veil is an ancient custom, although its origins are vague. It undoubtedly originated as an expression of sexual modesty. Many ancient peoples believed that the bride should be completely hidden from the prospective husband's gaze until after the marriage ceremony, and in some countries, this practice is still followed. The custom of wearing a bridal veil is old and cherished and contributes much to the romantic aura of a wedding. It probably became a permanently fashionable custom in the United States when Nelly Custis wore a long veil to her wedding to Major Lawrence Lewis, President George Washington's aide. She chose the veil because her fiancé had made appreciative comments about her appearance after glimpsing her through a lace curtain at an open window.

Along with the veil, most brides choose a white wedding dress, which tradition holds is a symbol of purity of mind and body and a sign of celebration.

Probably the most familiar wedding customs are contained in the following poem:

> *Something old,*
> *Something new,*
> *Something borrowed,*
> *Something blue—*
> *And a lucky sixpence in your shoe!*

Rare is the bride who ignores this old rhyme, which holds the promise of a lifetime of joy and happiness. An heirloom handkerchief, veil, or prayer book is often the "something old," and many brides wear pearls or another simple piece of jewelry that was worn by a mother or grandmother on her wedding day. By tradition, the "something new" is usually the wedding dress, some of its accessories, or the bridal bouquet. "Something borrowed" is frequently a handkerchief, gloves, or some accessory lent to the bride by one of her attendants or another close friend. "Something blue" is usually a blue garter, but it can also be a delicate blue monogram on the bride's slip, a small bow of blue ribbon attached to the inside of her gown, or another small accessory. A silver dime tucked into the bride's shoe serves as the "sixpence" that ensures good fortune. Frequently the dime is saved to be passed on to a daughter, godchild, or niece.

Orange blossoms are the traditional wedding day flower. The belief that orange blossoms bring extra assurance of happiness stems from the Roman myth that the goddess Juno gave Jupiter a "golden apple" on their wedding day. The English poets Spenser and Milton have interpreted the "golden apple" as an orange.

In fourteenth-century France, one was considered lucky to win the bride's garter. Everyone rushed for it at the end of the ceremony. So serious was this tradition that people were often hurt in the scuffle, and the wise bride soon learned to leave one garter dangling so it could be easily reached, and eventually the bride began to throw the garter.

Tossing the garter soon led to another custom, that of "stocking throwing," until brides began to rebel against a custom they considered undignified and embarrassing. Instead, they threw their bouquets, a custom that has persisted. Tradition holds that the person who catches the bouquet will be the next bride, so if you have someone special in mind (a sister or your maid of honor), you had better face the group and take careful aim. An impartial bride tosses the bouquet over her shoulder and leaves its recipient to fate.

When a woman was considered property and a price was paid for her, it was necessary for her father or guardian to give her—quite literally—to the groom. Today, the father walks his daughter to the altar and may give her in marriage as a sign of his approval of the union. In many ceremonies today, the father no longer gives away the bride or he does so on behalf of her mother and himself. The bride is never given away in a Catholic or Jewish ceremony.

Several traditions surround the prenuptial festivities. The first bridal shower is believed to have taken place in Holland when a father disapproved of his daughter's choice of a poor miller as a life partner. When the father forbade the marriage, her friends "showered" her with gifts so she would have the traditional dowry she needed to set up housekeeping.

At either a bridesmaids' party given by the bride or at a shower, a pink cake is traditionally served, with a ring, thimble, or coin baked into it. Legend holds that the woman whose piece of cake contains the trinket will be the next bride.

The bachelor party is a prevailing custom in many places today. Intended as a last fling, like the bridesmaids' party, it also provides an opportunity for the groom to thank his attendants and give them their gifts. Traditionally, the glasses used to toast the bride are tossed into a fireplace or otherwise broken so they can never be used for a less worthy purpose. If your fiancé plans to follow this custom, he should buy some inexpensive glasses for the purpose, or, at minimum, discuss these plans with the restaurant or club manager. Because of the amount of drinking that often takes place at the bachelor party, more and more grooms-to-be are holding this party two or three nights before their wedding day.

The trousseau, derived from the French word *trousse,* which means "bundle," originally was a bundle of clothes and housekeeping articles that the bride was expected to bring to her new home. Trousseaus expanded into dowries, which were often large enough to enhance the value of an unmarried daughter to her suitors. At one point, a trousseau was all the clothes a bride would need for one year, plus a generous amount of household linens—the finest the bride could afford. Today, a bride's trousseau usually consists of a few articles of new clothing picked for her honeymoon or her social needs in her new life.

The origin of the tiered wedding cake is particularly charming. In medieval England, a bride and groom kissed over a small pile of cakes. An enterprising baker soon massed these cakes together and frosted them, thus giving birth to the modern tiered wedding cake.

In ancient times, rice and other grains were symbols of fertility. The Romans broke a thin loaf of wheat bread over the bride's head, and the crumbs were eagerly sought after by the guests as good-luck tokens. Throwing rice—a custom that has sometimes given way to throwing confetti or rose petals—was the guests' way of wishing the couple a productive life with many children.

Along with rice, there was a time when old shoes were also thrown at a bride. The shoe was a symbol of possession and authority. When a woman married, her father gave one of her old shoes to the groom to signify that authority over her was now transferred to him.

The custom of throwing rice and shoes after the couple has now lost its original significance, and the throwing of rice and tying of shoes to the back of the couple's car remain only as symbols of good luck.

In ancient Rome, the doorstep or threshold was the domain of Vesta, goddess of the hearth, who is associated with virgins. One can well imagine what a bad omen it was if a bride stumbled while entering her new house, so it became traditional for the groom to carry her across the threshold. It is a pleasant custom that is followed even today, although the superstition associated with it has long been forgotten.

Throughout Europe, couples ride to and from church in horse-drawn carriages decorated with flowers and ribbons. In England, bells peal as the bride enters the church to be married and again as she leaves it with her husband. In Belgium, a bride carries a small handkerchief embroidered with her name. The handkerchief is framed until the next family bride carries it and has her name embroidered on it.

In Bermuda, the new husband plants a small tree in the yard of their home. Its growth is a symbol of their growing love for each other.

Honeymoons originated in the days of the ancient Teutons, when couples were married under a full moon and drank honey wine for thirty days following the ceremony, or until the moon waned. From this comes the custom of today's wedding trip.

There is a special place in the Bride's Organizer to record the traditions you keep at your wedding.

4

Who Pays for What

TALKING ABOUT MONEY

MONEY is a sensitive subject any time, but especially so when a wedding and two families who don't know each other well are involved. But the expenses of a wedding, which are never minor, must be discussed, and right away. Admittedly, this is where your dreams for your wedding may collide with the reality of what you can afford, but you have to know what you have to spend before you can begin planning your wedding, or for that matter, before you can even decide what kind of wedding you will have.

You will also have to settle whose money will be used to pay for the wedding. Traditionally, the bride's family has been expected to pay for almost everything, with the groom paying only for such personal items as the bride's rings, the wedding license, and the bride's bouquet. For the past few decades, though, the sharing of wedding expenses has been in a state of flux, largely because the costs of weddings have soared, and large, lavish weddings have become a burden to everyone but the very rich. In some parts of the country, it is now usual for the groom's family to give the rehearsal dinner. They also sometimes offer to pick up the tab for some other major wedding expense, such as the photography or the liquor. The bride and groom frequently pay for some, if not all, of their wedding these days, something they are able to do since people are marrying later when they are more established in their careers.

Generally, though, wedding expenses are broken down as follows:

Bride's (and her family's) expenses

1. The engagement photograph and announcement
2. Gifts from the bride to the groom, including his wedding band, and those given to her parents and bridesmaids
3. Flowers carried by the bridesmaids and flowers decorating the church and the reception
4. Musicians at the church and the reception
5. Aisle carpet and ribbons at the church or reception; canopy or tent or any other similar accessories
6. Wedding photographs
7. Lodging for bridesmaids, if necessary
8. Transportation for the wedding party to and from the wedding reception
9. All expenses connected with the reception, including food, beverages, and room rental
10. Invitations, announcements, and personal stationery for the bride
11. The bride's wedding clothes and her trousseau

The bride's family should make reservations for out-of-town guests but are not obliged to pay for their lodging. It is acceptable to find free accommodations with local friends and relatives.

Groom's (and his family's) expenses

1. The bride's engagement and wedding rings and her wedding gift, if there is one
2. The marriage license
3. Gifts for the best man and ushers and the groom's parents, if he chooses to give them something

4. Matching ties and gloves for the ushers
5. The bride's bouquet and corsage, flowers for the mothers and grandmothers, and boutonnieres for the men in the wedding party
6. The clergyman's fee
7. Overnight lodging for groomsmen if they come from out of town
8. The wedding trip

As a first step toward settling expenses, you and your fiancé should sit down alone to discuss the kind of wedding you hope to have. The groom, for example, may come from a very social family and expect a large, formal wedding. If you know this is beyond your family's means, say so frankly. Or you may know that your parents have been saving all their lives to give you a lavish wedding, and that they would be hurt if they could not do so. This, too, must be discussed.

The next step may be for each of you to talk to your families alone about the costs and expectations for this wedding. You should discuss the kind of wedding you would like to have, and ask your parents what they have in mind. If you plan to make a contribution, now is the time to mention it. In turn, the groom can similarly prepare his parents for the kind and size of wedding that they can expect. If they want a larger wedding than your family can afford, he can say this would be a burden on your family, and ask his parents if they are interested in contributing.

As soon as you have established what your parents expect to do, move quickly to include your fiancé and possibly even his parents, if they show any willingness to help out, in the discussion. Although the groom's parents may offer to pay for something, this should never be done in a way that offends your parents or suggests that they would not give a nice enough wedding. The bride's parents have the option of refusing or accepting any offer of assistance. If they decline his parents' offer of help, they should do so tactfully, saying, "Oh, we'd really like this to be our gift." The bottom line is that the bride's family should give the kind of wedding they can afford regardless of what the groom's family expect or could afford.

Unfortunately, the mere act of settling on a budget does not always banish all problems having to do with money. Additions to the guest list are the single item that most runs up the cost of a wedding. You may be pressured to add "just one or two more names." Stand firm, if you must, and say no. Once the budget has been established, stick to it even though doing so may require all your diplomatic skills. Neither you nor your parents (nor anyone else who is helping to pay for the wedding) should be pressured to spend more than she or he can afford.

Keep in mind, too, that this is your wedding and, within reason, you are entitled to have the kind you want. All contributions to your wedding expenses are gifts, and you should be grateful for them, but this still should not prevent you from deciding how the money will be spent. If you would rather have fewer floral decorations and ask more friends to the reception, that is your decision.

5
What Kind of Wedding

BAREFOOT brides and grooms are still getting married at sunrise (and sunset) on mountaintops and beaches, but for the most part the informality of the 1960s and early '70s has given way to more formal, elegant, and traditional weddings. About the only thing that has survived those casual decades is a taste for individualism. Brides today often want a wedding that bears their personal mark, one that is traditional with one or two untraditional touches.

The kind of wedding you have will, in large part, be dictated by what you can afford to spend. An elegant ultraformal wedding, which by definition means a large guest list, costs thousands of dollars. And although you can certainly plan an elegant, small wedding, simply by virtue of its being small, you will spend less.

For purposes of planning (and purchasing), your wedding will fall into one of several categories: ultraformal to formal, semiformal, informal, or last but hardly least, you may opt to have an intimate home wedding. Using these terms to describe your wedding will help everyone involved—the caterer, the florist, your wedding consultant—know what you have in mind.

The differences among the various kinds of weddings are described in detail on the following page but, generally speaking, the kind of wedding you choose dictates the size of the guest list, how the wedding party will be dressed, how many attendants you will have, what kind of invitations, and even how elaborate the food and entertainment will be.

ULTRAFORMAL TO FORMAL

This is a wedding with all the trimmings: a guest list in the hundreds (200 to 500 is usual); a traditional formal wedding dress with a train and a veil that is fingertip length or longer; the men in white tie or formal daytime wear; four or more attendants for each of you; formally worded, engraved or printed wedding invitations on plain white or ivory paper; elaborate floral decorations; and a reception, often at a private club or exclusive hotel or restaurant, that includes a sit-down dinner or multi-course buffet dinner and dancing to an orchestra or small band.

SEMIFORMAL

Most weddings are semiformal. The guest list usually numbers 100 to no more than 250. Your dress is traditional but has no train, and your veil is fingertip length or shorter. The men wear black tie or conservative dark suits; in summer they may opt for white dinner jackets. The invitations may be traditionally worded and engraved or printed on ivory or white paper, or they may use one of the newer wordings on pastel paper with some sort of artistic motif on the front. The wedding party usually consists of three or fewer attendants for each of you, and the reception, often held in a club, restaurant, hotel, motel, or wedding hall, varies from a sit-down meal to a buffet or afternoon tea. Music is typically provided by a small combo or a single musician.

INFORMAL

This is a small church or chapel wedding for 50 to 100 of your closest relatives and friends, with a reception held in the church parlor, at a restaurant, hotel, motel, or wedding hall. You wear a long or short wedding dress, or you may wear long or short street clothes, usually a pretty dress in a flattering color. Your veil is short (no longer than elbow length), or you may choose to wear a hat. You are attended by a maid or matron of honor and at most one bridesmaid; the groom has the same number of attendants. The men wear dark conservative suits or, occasionally, black tie. Invitations range from the traditionally worded, printed (rarely engraved) on white or ivory paper to the less traditional pastel colors; they may even be handwritten or telephoned. A light buffet lunch, dinner, or tea is served.

INTIMATE WEDDING

Many charming weddings are small affairs with only a few close friends and the immediate family. The ceremony takes place at city hall or the clergy's study, or it can be held at a restaurant or at home, although a home wedding does not necessarily have to be small. Depending upon the size of the house, a home wedding can be arranged for any number. You wear a pretty street-length dress with a hat and gloves, unless you are married at home. You do not wear gloves to be married in your own home, and you may wear a simple hat or go bareheaded. Nor does the mother-of-the-bride wear a hat or gloves in her own home.

At a small wedding, the bride typically has one or no attendants. Invitations are handwritten or telephoned, and the reception varies: it can be a simple afternoon tea, a buffet meal, or a sit-down dinner, whatever is desired and possible in the home setting.

Although the previous descriptions will help you begin to plan your wedding and talk with suppliers about it, the rules are not hard and fast. Brides planning a semiformal ceremony do occasionally wear dresses with trains or long veils if that's what they want. Certainly any bride getting married at home may wear a traditional white dress and veil if she wishes. If custom in your community or ethnic group dictates, an elaborate meal may be served at the least formal wedding. And while the informal and intimate home weddings are most appropriate for remarriages, second-time brides who did not have lavish weddings the first time sometimes like to pull out all the stops for their second weddings. This used to be frowned upon (even a white dress was frowned upon not too long ago for a remarrying bride), but I think no one should judge a couple harshly for wanting to celebrate a second or even a third marriage—especially since, if we think about it, these are marriages that we all hope will prove lasting.

Finally, brides today are often interested in adding some personal touch to their weddings—even at the expense of the "traditional" rules. I think this often makes for beautiful weddings, and I encourage it so long as whatever is done is within the bounds of good taste. For example, I've seen and heard of brides who have chosen to do the following:

☐ Wear an untraditional color. Color used to be relegated to the second-time or older bride, but today first-time brides are opting to add a smattering of it. I once talked with a bride who was planning to wear black—black velvet, to be specific. I thought this was a bit rebellious, but I love the idea of adding a touch of color, including red or black velvet, to a traditional wedding dress or headpiece. I believe this trend originated with rock singer Madonna's wedding dress, which had a filip of black on the headpiece, and I've seen several stunning designer wedding dresses that feature a bit of color.

    I've seen brides get married in sunflower blue and royal purple. Most instinctively steer away from red, but corals and pinks can be lovely. Less intimidating and more traditional is the wedding dress in a pastel tint. A bride who does not think she looks good in white (although there is a shade of white to flatter everyone) may want a pink- or blue-tinted dress.

☐ Wear an untraditional period dress. I'm not talking about the ubiquitous Victorian wedding dress that has been popular since the Princess of Wales chose this style for her wedding. Choose your own period, one that suits you. Most of us have a special historical era that we think we should

have been born into. Look into antique dresses and go for a
retro forties or even a fifties look. Choose to look like a
Spanish marquesa if you have the dramatic coloring and
looks to carry it off. If you're delicate and fair, think
Edwardian.

☐ For a formal, elegant wedding, wear a short dress, a mini,
but one with a long, trailing train that falls to the floor.

☐ Wear a stunning hat or headpiece that does not have a veil.
Usually brides who do not wear a veil wear flowers in their
hair, which is a lovely touch, but I'm thinking more of a
sophisticated, beaded or feathered headpiece. Of course, it
should match the mood of your dress.

☐ Go strapless. Once upon a time wedding dresses had to be
high-necked and long-sleeved. No longer. If you wear
something strapless or very low-cut, I do suggest wearing a
lace or organza cover-up for the ceremony, but you can doff
that once the reception begins.

☐ Wear two dresses. I attended a wedding where the bride
was married in a stunning full-skirted, floor-length lace and
taffeta gown. Somewhere between the first dance with her
father and the first course at dinner, she changed into a
very sophisticated, fitted, street-length lace dress that she
wore for the rest of the reception.

☐ Put the bridesmaids into something avant garde or
downright shocking. Hot pink minis with balloon skirts?
Fifties, floral prints? You're limited only by your
imagination. Black velvet? All these kinds of dresses and
many more are available these days.

☐ Add a witty touch to your wedding. The idea of writing
your own vows is less popular today and, besides, I believe
most brides want a traditional ceremony. But you can shake
everyone up with one untraditional touch, though, as did
the Atlanta bride who walked down the aisle in a perfectly
traditional dress preceded by perfectly traditional
bridesmaids to the tune of "Chapel of Love," a 1960's rock
hit. Needless to say, it was not a church wedding.

☐ Or take the couple, both Texans transplanted to New York,

who picked up their wedding guests in a school bus.
Everyone drank champagne and listened to
country-and-western music, the bride and groom's favorite,
while being driven to the wedding site in Central Park.

☐ Do something special with the reception colors and
decoration. I've seen black and silver look spectacular, also
white and red. In the former instance, black and silver
balloons were used for decorations, flowers were white, and
napkins were black. In the latter, white candles in silver
candelabra were surrounded by red roses.

☐ Explore other people's wedding customs. Have a French
croquembouche (a pyramid of cream puffs) rather than, or
along with, your wedding cake. Dance the hora or some
other folk dance at your wedding, even if you aren't Jewish.
Have a bevy of flower girls and pages, as the British do. If
your church or temple is nearby, walk to your wedding
with your wedding party as people do in many European
countries.

☐ Sometimes the untraditional will be dictated by
circumstances. Don't want to wait nine months for your
pregnant sister or best friend to have her baby? Let her be
your matron of honor anyway. Pregnant women never used
to attend brides, but assuming your sister or friend can still
walk gracefully (or assuming you really want her with you
and don't care how she walks), there's no reason that
pregnancy should rule out someone you love as an
attendant. I haven't seen this yet, but I've heard of two
instances where the "maid of honor" was a man—the
bride's closest friend. (He dressed like the rest of the men
in the wedding party.) I recently attended a wedding in
which the bride's mother, who had difficulty walking and
frequently used a wheelchair, was escorted down the aisle
by both her sons.

6

What Your Wedding Will Cost

IT is difficult to pin down the price of an "average" wedding because there are so many variables. A recent nationwide survey found that the average cost of a wedding today is between $12,000 and $19,000. A formal or ultraformal wedding is more expensive, especially in a large city. A few things can be said with certainty and, accordingly, can guide you as you think about the expenses of your own wedding: weddings are more expensive in cities than in smaller communities, and wedding receptions are more expensive in private clubs or fancy restaurants than in church parlors or at local motels.

The cost will also vary depending upon how you choose to purchase all the separate "elements" of your wedding. The biggest single expense is the reception. You can buy everything separately or purchase a "package" wedding of the kind that is offered by catering halls, restaurants, clubs, churches, and temples. Packages range from very basic—punch, tea sandwiches, taped music in the church parlor—to the very elaborate multi-course, sit-down dinner and full orchestra.

Many couples opt for at least a partial wedding package, if only to save time and energy. Typically, they buy the food and beverages as a package, and the music, cake, and flowers separately.

Buying everything separately is possible in theory but extremely wearing. You may save some money, but you will be frazzled from running around comparison-shopping, ordering everything, and worrying about whether all the deliveries will be made at the proper time and place. And ultimately, you may not save that much money. A catering hall, club, or restaurant can offer a competitive package price because it buys in quantity.

Cost of Reception

You may or may not be charged for the cost of a room for a reception, depending upon how many other services you use. Room costs vary from free to several hundred dollars per hour. Professional wedding planners say a reception should last from three to three-and-a-half hours. If it is shorter than this, the people who traveled a long distance will feel cheated, and if it is longer, people tend to break into cliques.

Whether or not you serve a meal depends upon your finances and what is expected in your community. For example, a sit-down dinner is served at Jewish weddings because of the custom of celebrating happy days with a hearty meal, and other ethnic and religious groups also traditionally serve a meal. If many of your guests have traveled very far, it is hospitable to feed them. And of course, if your wedding is held at a normal mealtime, people will expect it. If this will be a problem for you, consider inviting fewer people or changing the kind of reception you have—asking a few friends to cook for your reception, or cooking it yourself. Alternatively, plan a reception with light food, and then ask close family and out-of-town guests back to your mother's house for a heavier (usually buffet) dinner.

Cost of Food and Beverages

Costs for food and drink vary greatly, depending upon whether you serve chicken or steak, punch or imported champagne. In a city, expect to pay anywhere from $20 to $60 a person for a hot, cocktail buffet, $40 to $75 for a buffet dinner, and $50 to $150 for a sit-down dinner. Outside a large metropolitan area, costs are considerably less, and no matter where the wedding is held, you'll find a menu for every budget.

Caterer's estimates usually include the cost of beverages—typically a champagne toast, wine with dinner, and possibly mixed drinks—but be sure to check. Many caterers include the cost of champagne and wine, but charge extra for individual mixed drinks if you opt for an open bar. If you want an open bar—mixed drinks served at your guests' orders throughout the reception—you can either pay for the drinks individually or include them as part of the caterer's package.

Another way to save money is to buy the liquor yourself, thus saving 10 to 15 percent of the retail cost per case, and have it delivered to the reception. While in theory this saves money, in practice it is usually more trouble than it is worth. The last thing you'll want to be responsible for on your wedding day is making sure the liquor is delivered, counting what has been delivered as well as what is used, and then removing it from the reception premises after the party. Far better is to buy the liquor—all of it—from the caterer, who can usually offer you a reasonable price since he or she buys wholesale.

If you buy from the caterer or a wedding hall, be sure that everything is to your liking. For example, do you want expensive French champagne or one of the less expensive brands? True champagne comes only from one region of France, but there are some excellent non-French versions from Spain and the United States. The caterer can order whatever you want, down to the specific brand.

Do you want imported champagne served throughout the reception (expensive, compared to the cost of wine) or just for a champagne toast? Many people opt for a champagne toast only because it means they can afford a better champagne. If you do this, be sure the glasses are a generous size. No one will fault you for serving champagne in limited quantities, but it is stingy to serve it in small glasses. And do arrange for a second and even third glasses to be poured for those who like to toast a lot.

Check the same things about wine. Do you want domestic or imported? Here you're on more solid ground buying American, since there are many excellent, inexpensive domestic wines. Be sure the wine glasses are not stingy. And if you are going to serve wine, make sure you serve enough of it, not just one or two glasses per guest.

Mixed drinks are another matter, since they can add to the cost of a wedding—often in a highly unpredictable way. One bride's mother told me her guests drank three times more liquor at her younger daugher's wedding thann at her older daughter's. The reason: a blizzard that delayed the wedding for several hours and, she assumed, prompted a survival mentality on the part of those who made it to the wedding. Even if a blizzard does not strike before your wedding, serving mixed drinks that you pay for by the drink can be expensive.

It's better to buy mixed drinks with the package, if you can. The caterer will calculate that each guest will drink two or three mixed drinks and will price your package accordingly. You can lose if your guests are really light drinkers, but this rarely happens. If you know your guests will not drink much, this may be something to negotiate on the price of the package.

Find our how much liquor will go into each drink. While I don't think you need to serve the strongest drinks ever made, watered-down drinks are not very appealing. (A good way to decide what is appropriate is for you and your groom and possibly a few friends to sample the drinks.)

Other ways to cut costs on liquor are to serve punch or to dispense with mixed drinks. Punch is traditional at a wedding; and at a breakfast, lunch, or afternoon tea, no one should miss mixed drinks.

Cost of Wedding Stationery

The typeface, paper, size and number of enclosures determine the price of wedding invitations and announcements. Engraved invitations are more than double the cost of printed ones. Invitations can be purchased for as little as $75–$100 per 100 for simple printed ones, or as much as $600 per 100 for engraved invitations with response enclosures from a well-known jewelry store. Announcements cost the same as invitations.

Cost of Flowers

Flowers can easily become a major wedding expense if they are not kept simple. Perishable or out-of-season flowers will have to be ordered specially, a factor that adds to their cost. An elaborate bridal bouquet that requires lots of wiring to hold its shape will be more expensive than a small, simple arrangement. A bridal bouquet can cost anywhere from $25 to $250–$350. Bridesmaids' bouquets range from $20 to $125; boutonnieres, $5–$25; corsages, $8–$50. Decorative bouquets for the altar and reception cost $25–$250. Elaborate decorations can run into the hundreds and even thousands of dollars. The average cost of wedding flowers today is about $1,000.

Cost of Wedding Clothes

The average bridal outfit, including wedding dress, veil, shoes and other accessories, costs about $1,500. Wedding dresses range in price from $400 for a ready-made dress to several thousand dollars for a designer dress. Headpieces also run from $50 to several hundred dollars. A bride who is prepared to make her own dress and veil can spend considerably less. Attendants' outfits, which they usually pay for themselves, cost $100–$300. Rental formalwear for men averages $75–$100, except in large cities, where costs run higher.

Cost of Photographs

The money spent on photographs can vary from the cost of processing, if a friend takes them, to a professional album costing $1,000 or more. A two-hour videotape costs $600 and up. A typical wedding package includes an 8-×-10 of the bride and groom, two 5-×-7s, and ninety-six 3^1/$_2$-×-5s, plus an album, for a cost of $1,000.

Cost of Musicians

Most musicians must be paid union wages, which differ with the size and type of band but generally are no less than $200–$1,000 per hour for two to three musicians. An orchestra costs several thousand dollars, and an amateur soloist may cost as little as $50. The average amount spent on music for a 100-guest wedding is currently around $1,500.

Cost of Wedding Cake

Purchased separately from a baker, a cake that serves one hundred costs $150 to several hundred dollars. A home-baked cake or one made by a local amateur baker will cost less.

There are only rough estimates of average costs for the major items in a wedding reception. Remember that you must also buy brides-maids' gifts, arrange transportation for the wedding party on the day of the ceremony, and make a donation to the clergyperson and church musicians. There will also be miscellaneous extra expenses. It always pays to comparison-shop before you make final decisions, and to make this easier, the Bride's Organizer includes forms to help you keep a record of the estimates for various services. Also, remember that the purpose of the reception is to celebrate your wedding day with friends. A joyous occasion can be had just as well with homemade cake and simple punch as with an elaborate catered affair. A home or garden reception can be lovely and personal.

Here is a breakdown of the way wedding expenses are typically allotted.

Typical Breakdown of Wedding Expenses

Invitations and other stationery	6%
Photography	11%
Apparel	15%
Ceremony costs	11%
Reception costs	45%
Miscellaneous	12%

Tipping

In addition to the stated costs of a reception, you will also have to tip the people who serve you. The chart that follows shows the suggested amounts for tipping.

PERSON TIPPED	AMOUNT	WHO PAYS TIP
Caterer, hotel or club banquet manager, bridal consultant	10%–15%, only if special services are offered	Reception host adds any special payment to bill when he pays it
All servers, including waiters, waitresses, bartenders, and table captains	10%–15% for servers plus 2%–5% for captains if their fee is not included in the total bill	Reception host adds gratuities to bill when he pays it
Powder and coat-room attendants	$1 per guest to each attendant, or a flat fee can be arranged with the hotel or club manager	Reception host adds flat fee to bill when he pays it; otherwise, attendants are tipped right after reception.
Florist, photographer, baker, musicians, limousine drivers	15% for limousine drivers; 1%–15% for others only if special services are performed (delivery of flowers and cake is not usually considered a special service)	Limousine drivers should be tipped at the reception by host; other tips should be added to bill when paid

(Tipping continued)

PERSON TIPPED	AMOUNT	WHO PAYS TIP
Civil ceremony officials such as judges, justices of the peace, and city clerks	A flat fee (usually $25 is the minimum) is paid, but check first to see if the official can accept money	Groom pays via his best man after the ceremony
Clergyperson	Usually a donation based on his or her hourly income and dependent upon the time the clergyperson has spent with you and on the size of the ceremony	Groom pays, either at the last meeting or through his best man, who pays before or after the ceremony
Ceremony assistants such as altar boys and organists	$10-$50) The church often covers this fee, but check with the clergyperson to see what is appropriate	These tips are paid directly after the service by the wedding host
Custodians and kitchen help if the reception is held in the church	Ask the church secretary—these fees are usually set	

A DO-IT-YOURSELF RECEPTION

As wedding costs have soared, more and more brides have chosen to arrange their weddings themselves. Often they write their own invitations, make their own and their attendant's outfits, bake the cake, arrange the flowers, and prepare the food. Music can be provided by tapes. What a bride does not own, she can usually borrow for her reception—such things as silver serving pieces, candelabra, and serving tables. You can make your own tablecloths and decorate your home yourself. Such weddings are always charming, because they are so personal. They are also a wonderful way to save money. Chapter 12 is devoted entirely to planning and carrying out a home reception.

7
Scheduling Your Wedding

I'VE got to be honest with you: weddings take far more time to organize than you can possibly imagine before you embark on one. Unless you're prepared to move heaven and earth and work night and day on your wedding, three months is the minimum you need to plan anything but the most informal wedding. It's true, if you're willing to wear your best clothes and call your friends yourself to invite them, you can organize a very simple wedding in several days—but you'll still work around the clock and arrive at your own wedding with bags under your eyes.

Anything approaching a formal wedding takes six months or longer to plan. And if you want to marry in the popular months of June and August or if you live in a big city, you may find that twelve months is more like what you need. Society caterers, clubs and churches are typically booked a year in advance. Wedding dresses are sold in two seasons: fall-winter, for which gowns arrive in the stores in May, and spring-summer, for which they arrive in December. Wedding dresses are custom-ordered, which means that you try on samples. Your wedding dress will then be cut to your specific measurements and fitted to you after it arrives at the store or bridal shop—all of which takes a minimum of eight to twelve weeks. If you are on a shorter time schedule, you can sometimes buy a sample dress.

Actually, everything connected with a wedding is custom-ordered—the food and flowers, the bridesmaids' dresses, the invitations, even the napkins and matches. They all require time—yours to organize and decide what you want, possibly to comparison-shop, and the suppliers to make your products to order.

Your wedding will also take several months to plan because most brides work today, and in many instances, wedding plans must be fit in around their busy careers. If you are busy, you may need to allow even more time in which to plan and organize your wedding.

The best way to be on top of your wedding plans is to approach them in an orderly way. Use the schedules that follow to make sure everything gets done when it should. Call in advance for appointments with suppliers. They will appreciate your courtesy and set aside time to spend with you. On pages 198–199 of the Bride's Organizer, you will find a place to keep track of all the names, addresses, and appointments you will be making.

AS SOON AS POSSIBLE

1. Meet with the clergyperson to set a date; arrange for premarital instruction if necessary.
2. Draw up an overall wedding budget.
3. Decide on the formality, size, and location of your wedding and reception.
4. Decide on the number of guests, draw up your own guest list, and request a guest list from your parents and the groom's family.

SIX TO THREE MONTHS BEFORE THE WEDDING

1. Reserve the place for the reception.
2. Line up the caterer. Get lists of services and menu possibilities to look over before you make your final decision.

3. Book the musicians for the wedding and reception.
4. Ask the people you want to attend you if they will do so.
5. Order your invitations and announcements, also any other stationery you will need. Don't forget to order informals with your maiden name to use before the wedding and additional informals with your married name, if you are changing your name, to use after the wedding.
6. Meet with the florist, photographer, and baker.
7. If using Save the Date cards, prepare and send them.
8. Talk over honeymoon plans with your fiancé and make reservations as soon as you have decided where to go.
9. Shop for your wedding outfit and your attendants' outfits. Mothers should also be shopping for their dresses at this time.

TWO MONTHS BEFORE THE WEDDING

1. Firm up any last-minute arrangements for the menu, flowers, and wedding cake for the reception.
2. Begin to address invitations; they should be mailed no later than three weeks before the day of the wedding.
3. Register your preferences for gifts.
4. Select your wedding bands and order any engraving you want on them. Select your attendants' gifts.
5. Get your trousseau together. Buy any new clothes you will need and be sure clothes you already own are in perfect shape. Plan and if necessary, buy your going-away outfit.
6. Schedule and have the final fitting on your wedding dress and the attendants' dresses, if possible.
7. Have your wedding portrait taken.
8. Ask people to serve on the hospitality committee.

9. Double-check all arrangements. Call the caterer, baker, photographer, and florist to remind them and to confirm any last-minute changes. Make final selections for the music to be played at the wedding and reception and inform the musicians.
10. Put your financial affairs in order. Transfer or add your name to insurance policies, arrange bank and checking accounts, notify Social Security Administration, charge accounts, driver's license bureau, voter registration board, post office, clubs, etc., of your new name, if you are going to change it, and your new address.
11. Arrange lodging for out-of-town guests. Book and pay for any rooms for attendants.
12. Arrange transportation for out-of-town guests to and from airports, train stations, etc. (See pages 201–202 of Bride's Organizer.) Plan, too, for their entertainment.
13. Arrange transportation for all members of the wedding party to and from the ceremony and reception. (See page 200 of Bride's Organizer.)
14. Send maps showing the way from the church to the reception to out-of-town guests, but don't enclose these with the invitations.

FOUR TO SIX WEEKS BEFORE THE WEDDING

1. Order any special things you will need—candles, extra greenery, guest book, silver serving pieces, tables for reception, ashtrays. Check all details just as you would for any other party. Plan tablecloths for guests' tables and bride's table if this will not be taken care of by the caterer.
2. Pick up the marriage license; have any tests required by the state and a medical examination if you need one.
3. Make bags of rose petals or rice for tossing as you leave the reception.

4. Pick up any tickets or reservations needed for your honeymoon.
5. Plan the details of the rehearsal dinner and send invitations.
6. Plan the open house at your parents' home after the wedding. Usually this party is held for close friends and relatives immediately after the formal reception, but it may also be held the next day, particularly if a large number of out-of-town guests will be staying over.
7. Mail wedding invitations to guests.
8. Send the wedding announcement with your portrait to the newspapers at least three weeks before the wedding. (See page 203 of Bride's Organizer.)
9. Be sure your wedding outfit is in order—shoes dyed, jewelry selected, any special accessories ordered.
10. Make appointment for haircut and styling the morning of your wedding, or one or two days before it.
11. Arrange for a policeman to direct traffic at the church and reception sites.
12. Address wedding announcements.

ONE TO TWO WEEKS BEFORE THE WEDDING

1. Wrap gifts for attendants.
2. Pack for your honeymoon.
3. Give the reception manager or caterer a final estimate of the number of guests expected.
4. Make arrangements for wedding gifts, furniture, and personal belongings to be moved to your new home.
5. Make a final check with everyone concerned with the wedding to see that everything is in order.

Aside from the myriad details to be attended to, you will be attending parties in your honor and having the time of your lives being the center of attention. Enjoy yourselves!

8

Planning the Ceremony

THE planning of the ceremony should be one of the most meaningful activities of your wedding, involving both physical and spiritual preparation, but it too often gets lost in other events. If your clergyperson does not require several meetings with the two of you to help you work out the kind of ceremony you want, then you will benefit from taking time—perhaps over several long, leisurely dinners—to discuss what getting married means to you and what you want from your wedding ceremony. You need to discuss such things as the time of day you want to be married, whom you want for attendants, the kind of music you want, and your vows.

THE TIME OF DAY

Every religion has some holidays when marriages are not permitted or are discouraged, and most religions do not permit people to marry on their Sabbath. Your clergyperson will help you choose a suitable day.

Weddings are held in the morning, afternoon, and evening. A morning wedding can be held any time from 10 A.M., with a wedding breakfast afterward. Afternoon weddings are held at any hour, with 4:30 considered the most fashionable time. A tea reception follows. Dancing is making a comeback at afternoon weddings; it's a lovely custom, and I applaud it. A wedding held after 6 P.M. is followed by dinner and often dancing. Eight or 8:30, a popular time in the South (since the heat of the day has presumably burned off), is the latest hour that a wedding is held; weddings scheduled at this time often include a formal ball. Lavish cocktail food and a supper buffet or sit-down dinner are served.

CHOOSING THE ATTENDANTS

The number of attendants who make up your wedding party depends in large part on the kind of wedding you have. The more formal the wedding, the more attendants you will have, although this is not always the case. You can have a formal wedding with only one attendant if you choose to, although part of the beauty of a large, formal wedding is the sense of pageantry that comes from the processional and recessional.

The number of ushers depends upon the size of the guest list. One usher will be needed to seat every fifty guests. If there are more ushers than bridesmaids, only the number needed to pair up with the bride's attendants will actually walk in the processional and recessional.

Attendants may be single or married, and most religions now permit divorced persons to serve as attendants. (A divorced woman would be your maid of honor, not your matron of honor.) They are usually, but not necessarily, close in age to the bride and groom. Occasionally a groom will ask his father to be his best man, and although I've never seen a mother stand up for her daughter, I see no reason why this could not happen.

As for children serving as attendants to their parents who are remarrying, I heartily approve, provided the children are willing and comfortable doing so. A son may escort his mother down the aisle, and, for that matter, so may a daughter. Whether the child is officially a flower girl or a ring bearer, a maid of honor or an usher, or simply stands up at the altar with his parent does not matter. The point is for the child to feel a part of what is going on.

I have heard of one or two weddings where the bride has insisted on having a male attendant. While I think this would look odd, I can applaud the sentiment behind it. For the bride who is not interested in shocking her guests, I have a suggestion. If she is very good friends with a male other than her fiancé, she could ask her fiancé to include the man as one of his attendants. And conversely, today's modern bride should be prepared for her fiancé to ask her to include one of his close female friends among her attendants.

Attendants should always be close friends or relatives, because considerable expense is involved in being an attendant, and one may not refuse without a very good reason, such as absence from the country, another family commitment, or a recent death in the family. Call or write your attendants, or ask them in person. Be sure to specify the date and time of the wedding and the degree of formality. If an attendant cannot afford to accept (attendants generally pay for their outfits and their transportation to and from the wedding), one hopes he or she will feel comfortable enough to discuss this directly rather than making up an excuse that will cause him or her to miss the wedding entirely. The bride or groom or the family may then offer to pay the expenses, although this must be done with the utmost tact when only one attendant is involved. If a friend truly cannot afford to be in a wedding, perhaps some other honorary position or role, such as an assigned reading during the ceremony, might be arranged for him or her.

An invitation to participate in a friend's wedding should not be accepted—or declined—lightly. If you must decline, do so with sincerest and most tactful regrets. Make the bride or groom feel that you truly would like to be part of such an important, meaningful day if it were at all possible.

Once attendants have been invited to participate, they are treated as honored guests. They—and their spouses or dates—receive invitations to the wedding, rehearsal dinner, and any other festivities that surround the wedding. The exception is showers. If these are numerous, a thoughtful bride will invite her attendants to only one or two showers or will indicate to them that either no gift or only a very small gift is expected after the first party.

In the Bride's Organizer you'll find a place for the names, addresses, and phone numbers of all your attendants.

THE BRIDE'S ATTENDANTS

The bride is attended by a maid or matron of honor, who is her main attendant, one or more bridesmaids or junior bridesmaids, and a flower girl (or girls), if she chooses.

Maid of Honor

The maid of honor is usually the bride's sister, a cousin, or her closest friend. If the person is married, she is called the matron of honor. The maid of honor is the bride's personal attendant during the ceremony. She lifts the bride's veil, holds her bouquet during the ceremony, and keeps the groom's ring, if there is one. She may be distinguished from the bridesmaids by a slight variation in the style or color of her dress or by slightly different flowers. Or her outfit and flowers may be the same as those of the bridesmaids.

Bridesmaids and Junior Bridesmaids

Bridesmaids are generally about the same age as the bride and are her close friends, although she frequently invites a cousin to whom she is close and a relative, usually a sister, of the groom.

A junior bridesmaid is usually a sister or cousin under the age of sixteen and as young as ten or eleven. Her duties are exactly the same as the other bridesmaids—to be a lovely and joyous addition to the wedding party and to mingle with the guests during the reception.

Bridesmaids pay their own expenses to and from the wedding; lodging is usually arranged for and paid by the bride's family. Bridesmaids purchase all of their outfits except for the flowers, which are provided by the bride's parents. It is perfectly acceptable for the bride's parents to pay for the expenses for any or all of the bridesmaids.

Flower Girl

A bevy of flower girls, à la British custom, is delightful and will, I suspect, be seen more often in the future. Although a flower girl can be any little girl from age four to eight, maturity and poise should be determining factors in your selection. A child who is shy or frightened may balk at the moment when she has to walk down the aisle or may cause some disturbance during the ceremony. The flower girl, usually a sister, cousin, or niece of the bride or groom, carries a small bouquet or scatters rose petals as she goes down the aisle. Her dress is anything appropriate for a young child that is in keeping with the color and style of the wedding.

THE GROOM'S ATTENDANTS

The groom selects a best man, ushers, and possibly a small boy as ring bearer.

Best Man

Thought should be given to the selection of the best man, as he will more or less be the mastermind on the day of the wedding. The best man, usually the groom's brother or close friend, and sometimes his father or a grown son, calls for the groom on the day of the wedding, helps him dress, and accompanies him to the wedding. He makes sure the ushers are properly dressed and versed on their duties; he carries the wedding ring in a convenient place so he can produce it, with a minimum of fumbling, at the proper moment. He pays the minister, and he may carry such items as the bride and groom's car keys, their travel tickets, and their marriage license. During the reception, he generally offers a toast to the bride and groom; often he is expected to initiate the toasts.

Ushers

Ushers, selected by the groom from among his close friends and relatives or from the bride's relatives, are part of the bridal procession.
They escort guests as they arrive and exit.

The ushers, like the bridesmaids, should show concern for the com-
fort of the guests. Unattended women should be asked to dance by the
ushers.

Groomsmen provide their own clothing, either purchased or rented,
although matching ties and gloves may be provided by the groom as
a gift to his attendants. Out-of-town attendants are expected to provide their own transportation, although the father of the groom or the
groom may offer to pay for outfits and transportation for one or all of
the groomsmen. Flowers for the groomsmen are provided by the
groom's parents or the groom. Arrangements for lodging are usually
made and paid for by the groom; attendants can stay with close friends
or relatives or in a hotel.

Ring Bearer

A ring bearer, who can be any boy from about four to seven years old
who has the social poise to handle the occasion, walks in the processional and carries the ring, securely sewn on a small white pillow. His
outfit is similar to or the same as those of the groomsmen, or he may
wear short pants or something of his own that is in keeping with the
formality of the wedding.

Some special attentions are necessary for the ring bearer and flower
girl. They and their parents are invited to the rehearsal dinner, and
special arrangements for their transportation should be made. As a
remembrance, each child should be given a small gift and a photo
should be taken with the bride and groom.

THE UNOFFICIAL ATTENDANT

Contributing to the overall success of the wedding and reception
should be some kind of supervisor-general, usually an aunt, older
sister, godmother, or good and trustworthy friend. These days this

person is often a paid professional, the wedding consultant. Such a person can graciously handle the details of the receiving line, signal the time to cut the cake, make the toasts, start the music for the first dance, remind others of the order of dances, and see that pictures are taken of everyone the bride and groom want pictures of. The person who graciously accepts your invitation to oversee the wedding should make things run smoothly and should be given complete charge, but she should take care not to upstage the mother of the bride, who is the official hostess. This person should be given a gift and a photo should be taken of her with the bride and groom.

MUSIC DURING THE CEREMONY

Since the music played before and during the processional and recessional can set the entire tone of the wedding ceremony, you will want to take care to select music you truly enjoy, music that is in keeping with the religious significance of the wedding. When you meet with the clergyperson, ask for his or her views on music that is suitable. Then plan to meet with the musicians for the wedding and the reception. Discuss the music you want played; listen to them play or sing part or all of it, and decide what you would like played and in what order. For the ceremony, about fifteen to thirty minutes of music are planned for the time when guests are arriving, and a march is needed for the processional and the recessional. Select music that you and your groom appreciate; you need not necessarily take the advice of others if it is contrary to what you want.

If the musical program is complicated, a full rehearsal may be in order. If you have hired professionals, the church's regular musicians, or students from a nearby musical school, some payment is expected. If the musicians are friends, gifts are in order.

Favorite selections for music prior to the ceremony include *Arioso* by Bach, Preludes on Antiphone by Dupré, Aria in F Major by Handel, but can be any other music you particularly like. A favorite song of the betrothed couple may be played or sung. If a vocalist is used, he or she sings about ten to fifteen minutes before the ceremony and again just before the mother of the bride is seated.

Processional music should be joyous, yet dignified. The entrance music as the bride begins her walk down the aisle is traditionally the bridal chorus from Wagner's *Lohengrin,* but other popular processionals include the Air from the Water Music Suite by Handel, Trumpet Voluntary in D by Purcell, and Rigaudon by Campra. The music is played softly as the attendants come down the aisle, and changes in content or volume to announce the bride. Background music is sometimes played softly during the vows, but you should check with the clergyperson before making plans for this.

Recessional music is quicker in tempo and livelier than the processional. Popular recessionals are the Wedding March from *Midsummer Night's Dream* by Mendelssohn, Ode to Joy from Symphony No. 9 by Beethoven, and Trumpet Voluntary in D by Purcell. In recent years, the Mendelssohn wedding march has been frowned upon by purists who feel that it is not in keeping with the religious nature of the service. Such opinions do not seem to have hindered its popularity, and if you want it and your clergyman agrees, have it played. It is your wedding.

Increasingly today, nonreligious music is heard at weddings. Many couples have a favorite song and want to incorporate it into the ceremony. Whether or not you may do this depends entirely upon the clergyperson who will officiate at your wedding. Some frown on anything but nonsecular music as part of the service, while others are open to other choices. When choosing the music, try to select something that has innate dignity and will stand the test of time. That way, your clergyperson will be more inclined to accept it.

There is such a wide variety of possible music that you may find yourself confused. If so, a trip to the library or a local music store where you can listen to recordings is in order. Most libraries have collections of fine music that can be checked out. A call to a high school or college music teacher or the church organist can also unearth some helpful information.

You should not feel embarrassed at not knowing what music is appropriate, nor should you be afraid to take your doubts to people whose business is to know. They will be glad to help you.

Generally a month should be allowed between the final selection of the music and the ceremony. In the Bride's Organizer, you'll find a place to write out a list of the music chosen and the order in which you would like it played. Give one copy to the musicians and keep one for yourself.

You may want to spend a little time practicing walking to the music you have chosen. If possible, obtain a record of the music and play it frequently to become accustomed to it. Wedding music is highly emotional, and many brides have cried their way to the altar because of the sudden effect the music has had on them. It might also be a good idea to tell your father you need to practice walking on his arm to the music and give him a chance to get used to it, too. Elaborate wedding walks are unpopular today, but a lovely bride will want to have an aura of confidence about her ability to float down the aisle to the music she has chosen.

Music is, of course, as important to the reception as to the ceremony, and reception music is discussed in chapter 11.

PLANNING YOUR VOWS

Your religion and your clergyperson's preferences will have much to do with the kind of vows you exchange. If you want to write your own vows or do anything untraditional, you need his or her approval to do so. Most clergypersons are delighted to counsel a bride and groom who are seriously interested in making their vows personal and meaningful.

Although there has been a return to the traditional wedding ceremony, not everything is old-fashioned. Many women today, for example, object to the promise to obey their future husbands, and this phrasing is often omitted from the vows, or the word *respect* is substituted and used by both bride and groom.

Some women are uncomfortable being "given" in marriage by their fathers. One solution has been for the father to respond, "Her mother and I do," when asked who gives the woman in marriage; some brides prefer to skip this part of the ceremony entirely, in which case their fathers escort them down the aisle and then join their mothers in the front pew without saying anything. Another trend is for both parents to escort their daughter down the aisle—although this is hardly a new trend, since Jewish parents have escorted their children down the marital aisle for many years.

Some couples also object to the promise to love "until death do us part," preferring to substitute what they view as a more realistic phrase, "so long as we both shall love."

Couples who wish to write their own vows entirely must do so with the help and approval of the clergyperson, who should also be able to guide them. Many couples wish simply to have a special reading or poem as part of the wedding ceremony. They may read it to each other, ask the clergyperson to read it, or honor a friend by asking him or her to do so. Anthologies of poetry can provide some sources, and there is the perenially popular *Prophet* by Kahlil Gibran. An excellent source of quotable material is the Bible. Use a concordance or ask your clergyperson to help you locate relevant verses.

With so many ceremonies being personalized, some brides and grooms are choosing to have a printed program of their wedding—a keepsake for their guests. These are placed on the chairs or in the pews before the wedding guests arrive. If you decide to do this, as soon as you and the clergyperson have planned the ceremony write up the program and get it to a printer so it can be ready well in advance of the ceremony. Most instant printers can handle an order like this within one week.

Before planning your ceremony, you may also want to read chapter 19, which describes the wedding ceremony in various religions.

9
Invitations and
Announcements

WHOM TO INVITE

ONCE you have chosen the date, time, and place of your wedding, it is time to begin preparing a guest list. If your wedding is to be large enough for you to invite everyone you want to, lucky you. If not, you will have to do a little tactful sorting out. First on your list will probably be relatives, followed by close family friends, the people who have watched you grow up and participated in your life at other meaningful stages. You will also want to include your dear friends—and your mother will want to include her dear friends, and the groom's mother will have a similar list. The clergyperson and his spouse are invited to the wedding and reception, as are the husbands and wives of married attendants. It's especially nice, if you can afford to do so, to give your attendants the option of bringing a date. When two people live together, they also must be invited together even though you may only know one partner. The parents of the flower girl and ring bearer are invited to the wedding and reception. Parents of un-married attendants are invited to the wedding and reception, if they live nearby. Technically, the bride and groom share the list equally—that is, each invites half the guests. Some names will be added to the list jointly by you and your fiancé. If your fiancé's family lives far away, it is probably perfectly all right for you to take a larger share of the guest list. Otherwise, you will have to do whatever negotiating is required.

To be sure you haven't forgotten someone dear to you, make a last-minute check through your address book and your old Christmas card lists as well as those of your parents; go through alumni directories and club membership lists, too, to see if there is anyone you have missed.

Often there are some fuzzy areas on guest lists—people you aren't sure whether or not to invite. Usually these are people with whom you or your fiancé work, neighbors who are friends only by virtue of proximity, and out-of-town friends. If your guest list is small, you probably won't ask any of these people. Sometimes, when the guest list is limited, it is better not to ask anyone from a group—the people you work with, for example—than to ask only some of the people. If you have a co-worker to whom you feel especially close though, by all means include him or her. On the one hand, out-of-towners will probably be flattered to be asked to your wedding if they're close friends, even if they can't attend. On the other hand, since an invitation obligates people to send a gift, you may want to send announcements instead to out-of-town friends if you know they cannot possibly attend your wedding.

WHAT KIND OF INVITATION?

If your wedding is very small—just the immediate families and a few friends—you will probably invite people by calling or writing them personally. Either you or your mother as the official hostess can issue these informal invitations.

Formal, semiformal, and even some informal wedding invitations are usually printed or engraved. Either way, their preparation requires several weeks—only a couple of weeks if you use an instant printer and up to three months if you go to a popular engraver. If you want to get a head start on preparing your invitations, ask the printer if the envelopes can be sent to you as soon as possible so you can start addressing them. That way you can have them addressed and ready to mail as soon as the invitations are printed. Don't forget, too, to order several extra invitations as keepsakes for you, your mother, and your groom's mother—and to cover mistakes.

You may address your invitations yourself or hire a professional calligrapher to do so, at a cost of about $1 per invitation. Calligraphers are listed in the phone book, as are printers and engravers.

When you are choosing your invitations, the printer or engraver will show you samples of types and papers. Wedding invitations are usually set in a rather traditional script typeface, although many brides prefer a more modern typeface. Below are several typefaces that are excellent for invitations.

Mr. and Mrs. Michael Frank Natale

Mr. and Mrs. William H. Weissler

Mr. and Mrs. Richard G. Manning

Mr. and Mrs. Benjamin Getz

Mr. and Mrs. Michael Anthony Napolitano

Mr. and Mrs. Nathan L. Gruskoff

Mr. and Mrs. Vincent J. Vitolo

WORDING THE FORMAL INVITATION

Formal wedding invitations are traditionally issued by the parents of the bride, although there is a trend toward having both parents issue them. Another trend is for the couple to issue the invitations themselves. Usually a signal that they are paying for their own wedding, couples who choose to do this are typically older and more established, and the wedding often takes place where they live rather than in the bride's hometown. Couples also issue their own invitations for a second or third marriage.

The wording of a formal wedding invitation, which, by the way, can be used for a formal, semiformal, or informal wedding (and may even be handwritten in blue or black ink on white or ivory paper), follows a specific format, one that has been used for many years.

The type is centered on the page, and punctuation and capitalization follow the format shown in the samples. Except for titles, abbreviations are not used. Titles—*Mr., Mrs., Dr.*—are used by the parents and the groom, but these days, in a move toward egalitarianism, the trend is to dispense entirely with titles, especially in some situations. The title *Ms.* seems not yet to have made its way into wedding invitations. For example, a very traditional invitation would read:

at the marriage of their daughter
Joan Elizabeth
to
Mr. John Hawkes

but it might also read:

at the marriage of their daughter
Joan Elizabeth
to
John Hawkes

When both parents are doctors, the easiest thing may be to dispense entirely with titles. If the woman does use her title socially, she is Dr. Joan James and not Dr. Henry James, and the invitation will read:

Dr. Joan James and Dr. Henry James
request the honour of your presence

Or if she is a physician and her husband is not, it reads:

Dr. Joan James and Mr. Henry James

When either the bride and groom or both are doctors, their invitation uses their titles accordingly:

Dr. Amy Fremion
and
Mr. Greg Chapelle
request the pleasure of your company

One helpful trick with difficult invitations is to try to keep everything parallel, as in the above example where titles are used for both the bride and groom. Alternately, no titles could be used for either one. Also, use full names; nicknames are inappropriate on a formal invitation.

The hour and the year (the latter is optional) are spelled out:

four o'clock
nineteen hundred ninety-one

A.M. and P.M. are not used with the hour since this is obvious. An eight o'clock wedding always refers to eight P.M. and a ten o'clock wedding to ten A.M. The city and state are spelled out, too. *New York City* is traditionally used in place of *New York, New York,* and with other major cities such as San Francisco, Los Angeles, and Chicago, the state may be omitted.

If both parents are living and still married to each other and this is your first marriage, your invitation will read:

Mr. and Mrs. Henry Robert James
request the honour of your presence
at the marriage of their daughter
Barbara Ann
to
Mr. Ronald John Borkgren
on Saturday, the third of June
at three o'clock
Visitation Church
Four hundred ten West Central Boulevard
Kewanee, Illinois

The church street address may or may not be included on the invitation. If it is, it should be spelled out. The year can be left off the invitation, but should be included on the announcement of the marriage. The word *honour* is usually spelled with the *u*.

Both Sets of Parents Issue Invitation

I like the idea of including the parents of the groom on the wedding invitation. Before issuing such an invitation, though, the parents of the bride or the bride herself should check with the groom's parents to be sure they are comfortable being included. If they are not, they should feel free to decline. A joint invitation would read as follows:

Mr. and Mrs. Henry James

and

Mr. and Mrs. Tyson Williams

request the honour of your presence

at the

marriage of their children

Barbara Ann James

and

Ronald John Williams

on Saturday, the third of June

nineteen hundred eighty-nine

at three o'clock

Visitation Church

Four hundred ten West Central Boulevard

Kewanee, Illinois

Engaged Couple Issues Invitation

When a couple issues their own invitation, it should read:

Mary Ann Foxx

and

William Harlan

request the honour of your presence

at their marriage

on Saturday, the sixth of October

nineteen hundred eighty-nine

at four-thirty

Central Presbyterian Church

Thirty Elm Street

Columbus, Indiana

Other Relative Issues Invitation

When an invitation is issued by someone other than the bride's parents, the relationship is usually mentioned (at the marriage of their niece, their granddaughter, her sister). In the rare event that the groom's parents issue an invitation (usually because the bride is from another country and has no close family nearby to issue invitations for her), no relationship to the bride is mentioned (because there is none yet), but the invitation reads:

at the marriage of
Jacqueline Suzanne
to their son
James Humphrey

Divorced Parents Issue Invitation

These days women's names are in a state of transition. Until a few years ago, a divorced woman used a combination of her maiden name and her ex-husband's surname. Thus Mary Browne, née Mary Jones, upon divorcing became Mrs. Jones Browne. Gradually, this has given way to a more popular usage, Mrs. (or Ms.) Mary Browne, and, of course, many divorced women take back their maiden names. I think a woman should use whatever name she is known by and personally prefers on her or her child's wedding invitation.

An invitation may be issued jointly by divorced parents if that is the bride's preference. If her mother has remarried, it would read:

Mrs. William Eugene Stewart
and
Mr. Jack Davison Young
request the honour of your presence
at the marriage of their daughter
Jacqueline

If the bride's mother has not remarried, it should be issued as follows, using her maiden name and your father's name:

Mrs. Walsh Stewart (or:) *Mrs. Mary Stewart*
and
Mr. William Stewart
request the honour of your presence

If the bride has been divorced and her parents are sponsoring the wedding, the invitation should read:

Mr. and Mrs. Charles James Hughes
request the honour of your presence
at the marriage of their daughter
Jean Hughes Brown

Bride Divorced or Widowed

If the bride is widowed and her parents are sponsoring the wedding, the invitation should read:

Mr. and Mrs. Charles James Hughes
request the honour of your presence
at the marriage of their daughter
Jean Louise Smyth

If the bride has been divorced and is sponsoring her own wedding, the invitation should read:

The honour of your presence
is requested at the marriage of
Mrs. Hughes Brown (or:) *Mrs. Jill Brown*
(or:) *Jill Brown*

If the bride is widowed and is sponsoring her own wedding, the invitation should read:

The honour of your presence
is requested at the marriage of
Mrs. David Michael Brown

Double Wedding Invitations

Sometimes two sisters or good friends are married in the same ceremony. Sisters usually issue joint invitations, and friends may or may not choose to do so. The older woman's name usually appears first on the joint invitation. Sample invitations follow:

Mr. and Mrs. Charles James Hughes
request the honour of your presence
at the marriage of their daughters
Jean Louise
to
Mr. William Keith Summers
and
Joan Marie
to
Mr. Stanford Gerald Forrest

A joint invitation of friends would read:

Mr. and Mrs. Harry H. Blancher
and
Mr. and Mrs. Ronald Dewitt
request the honour of your presence
at the marriage of their daughters
Stacy Marie Blancher
to
Mr. Richard Harold Smith
and
Amy Ann Dewitt
to
Mr. Steven Michael Brown

Military Invitations

When the bride or groom is a commissioned officer in the United States armed forces, the invitations and announcements give his or her title. If the officer's rank is lieutenant colonel or above in the army, commander or above in the navy, Merchant Marine, or Coast Guard, or major or above in the Marine Corps, the title is used before the name:

Colonel William Cullen Bryant Stewart
United States Army

Mention of the branch of service is optional.

If the bride or groom holds a rank in the army below those described, the name appears on a single line with the title set separately on the line below:

William Cullen Bryant Stewart
Second Lieutenant, United States Army

If the bride or groom holds a rank below that of commander in the navy, the rank also appears on a single line:

Mary Joan Bryant Stewart
Lieutenant, junior grade, United States Navy

If a graduate is married the day of or a few days after receiving his or her commission from Annapolis, West Point, or the U.S. Air Academy, he or she may use the rank on the wedding invitation.

A new reserve officer receiving a commission and awaiting the commencement of his or her obligated training tour cannot use the rank and branch designation on wedding invitations or have a military wedding in uniform. This regulation pertains to the period between graduation and the assignment to active duty, which may be several weeks or months. He or she may properly be identified, however, by rank and branch designation if, as a new reserve officer, he is, in fact, on active duty at the time of the wedding.

Retired high-ranking army and navy officers may retain their titles in civilian life:

Commodore William Cullen Bryant Stewart
United States Navy, Retired

Or:

Lt. General William Cullen Bryant Stewart
United States Marine Corps, Retired

Unless retired or inactive reserve officers are colonels or above, their former titles may not be used.

Noncommissioned officers and enlisted personnel use only their names with the branch of service immediately below, and *Mr.* or *Miss* is omitted before the name:

> *Dr. and Mrs. James B. Hopping*
> *request the honour of your presence*
> *at the marriage of their daughter*
> *Erin Marjabelle*
> *to*
> *William Cullen Bryant Stewart*
> *United States Marine Corps*

INFORMAL INVITATIONS

When a small wedding is held on short notice and there is neither time nor the need for printed or engraved invitations, informal invitations may be issued by telegram, telephone, or in a personal note from the bride's mother or the bride. As noted earlier, any invitation to a wedding, no matter how small or informal, can be written with the formal wording, but usually when an intimate wedding is planned, a more intimate invitation is also sent:

> *Dear Sue and Bill,*
>
> *Rusty and Jackie are being married quietly at the house on Saturday, September 19, at 2:30. We do hope you will be able to attend and will also stay for dinner afterward. We're looking forward to sharing this joyous occasion with you.*
>
> *Love,*
> *Rosie*

Nontraditional Informal Invitations

Another kind of invitation that is seen more and more often these days is what I call, for lack of a better description, the nontraditional invitation. Used for semiformal and informal weddings, such invitations are informal by virtue of their design and wording. They may be printed on colored (usually pastel) paper, and often feature a poem, drawing, or motif of some sort on the cover. They also often feature a nontraditional wording, the most common being:

> *We invite you to share with us our joy in the marriage of our daughter, Sandra Louise, to John Michael Smyth. Their vows will be said on Saturday, the second of July, at four-thirty o'clock, at Christ Episcopal Church, Danville, Illinois.*
>
> *After the worship service, we hope you will be our guests at the reception that will follow at the Danville Country Club.*
>
> *Louise and Samuel Montgomery*

In planning such invitations, care must be taken that they are tasteful. Garish colors, sentimental poems, and the like should be avoided. I see no reason for people not to issue nontraditional invitations, however, if they want to.

Invitations Through a Newspaper

Although many urban newspapers no longer announce all weddings and engagements, most small-town newspapers continue this tradition. When a newspaper permits it, the invitation can be included in the engagement notice. The last line of the announcement might read:

> *No invitations are being sent, but all friends and relatives of the couple are invited to attend the wedding and reception.*

If the wedding is to be private, in some communities that fact also should be announced in a newspaper story. To ensure privacy, sometimes the time and place of the wedding are withheld until they are printed in the wedding announcement.

When only a small reception is planned and the wedding invitation has been issued through the papers, it is more tactful not to mention the reception at all.

If you decide to announce your wedding and invite guests in this manner, it is a good idea also to send notes to people you especially want to attend. If notes are sent, they are handwritten on heavy white paper in black or dark blue ink. (Alternately, printed invitations may be issued.) They should be issued by the mother or parents of the bride or on her or their behalves and should follow the same wording as the informal invitation on page 66.

INVITATION ENCLOSURES

The Reception Card

If the reception will be held immediately after the wedding in the church, this information is included on the wedding invitation. A joint wedding-reception invitation reads this way:

Mr. and Mrs. John Davison Young
request the honour of your presence
at the marriage of their daughter
Jacqueline
to
Mr. E. Russell Anderson
on Saturday, the seventeenth of September
at ten o'clock
First Congressional Church
Silver Spring, Illinois
and afterward at breakfast
at Midland Country Club

R.S.V.P.
312 Quaint Acre's Drive
Silver Spring, Illinois 61443

Alternately, you can enclose a separate reception card. About half the size of the invitation, it is identical in type, paper, and printing style to the invitation.

A card announcing a reception held in the bride's home would read:

Reception
immediately following the ceremony
522 South Tremont
Kewanee, Illinois 61443
R.S.V.P.

The card for a reception held in a club or hotel would read:

Reception
immediately following the ceremony
The Midland Country Club
R.S.V.P.
522 South Tremont Street
Kewanee, Illinois 61443

A separate reception card is used when only some of the guests at the wedding are invited to the reception.

If a meal is to be served at the reception, this may be noted on the invitation. If the reception is a luncheon or dinner, you can add the words *and luncheon* or *and dinner*.

If it is a breakfast, the following form might be used:

Mr. and Mrs. John Davison Young

request the pleasure of your company

at the wedding breakfast of their daughter

Jacqueline

and

Mr. E. Russell Anderson

on Saturday, the third of June

at one o'clock

Creve Coure Club

Peoria, Illinois

R.S.V.P.

312 Quaint Acre's Drive

Silver Spring, Illinois 61443

Note that the expression *honour of your presence* has been changed on the reception card to *pleasure of your company*. When a wedding is held in a house of worship, the *honour of your presence* is correct. When the ceremony is held elsewhere, such as in a club, restaurant, or hotel, the expression *pleasure of your company* is used on the wedding invitation, even if a separate reception invitation is enclosed.

Response Cards

For many years a response card tucked inside a wedding invitation was considered an insult, since well-mannered persons always responded to their invitations. As it turns out, in our busy world, some people fail to take the time to reply to invitations, hence the need for a response card. Few of us today would risk inviting people to a major party like a wedding reception without using the extra prod of such a card, and even so I constantly hear from brides that they or their mothers still have to make last-minute calls to ask whether people are coming. If you feel, however, that a response card will offend anyone on your guest list, simply do not enclose one with that invitation.

Response cards, which should match the invitations, are ordered at the same time. They come in their own small envelopes, preprinted with a return address. If the bride's parents are giving the wedding, their address is used. If the bride and groom are giving their own wedding, the envelopes are printed with the bride's name. They are not printed with both your names even if you have been cohabiting for years. If possible, put a stamp on each return envelope, which means response cards will double the cost of postage. If your budget is really tight, you may skip the stamp.

The best form for a response card is as follows:

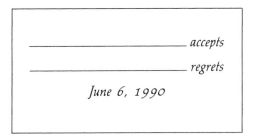

The date on the card is that of your wedding. Only if you must have an unusually early response (the caterer insists on knowing the head count a month in advance) should you give people a deadline for responding.

An alternate form of the response card is:

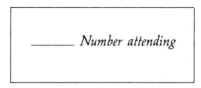

But this leads to confusion, because some people think they are to fill in the number of people attending and may include children and other family members whom you have not intended to invite. You may find yourself with unexpected guests.

At-Home Cards

If you will be moving into a new home after your wedding and want to notify people of your new address, order at-home cards to enclose with your invitations and announcements. They might read like this:

At home
after the sixth of June
1255 North Lake Shore Drive
Chicago, Illinois 60611

Or this:

Mr. and Mrs. Harold Brown
after the tenth of August
300 Riverside Drive
New York City 10025

Church Cards

When a wedding is very large or the persons being married are promi-nent and want to keep out reporters and other uninvited persons, church cards are sometimes issued with the invitations. They are printed on paper in the same type as the wedding invitations, and should read:

Please present this card
at Visitation Church
on Saturday, the sixth of June

A more old-fashioned but thoughtful custom at a large wedding is another kind of church card that ensures that close relatives and family friends will be seated near the front of the church. These cards may be printed, or you may purchase suitable cards to write on or use the bride's mother's informals. Such cards consist of a handwritten note saying, *Within the ribbons, Bride's reserved section,* or *Groom's reserved section.* Guests should carry them to the wedding and hand them to an usher.

ANNOUNCEMENTS

Those who are not invited to a wedding, either because they live far away and could not attend or because the number of guests invited to the wedding was limited, are usually informed through an announcement that the wedding has taken place.

Announcements, similar in shape, size, and form to invitations, are sent after the wedding has taken place. They can be mailed after any kind of wedding, even an elopement.

The wording of an announcement is only slightly different from that of a wedding invitation. The year is always included, even if it did not appear on the invitation, and the name of the church may be left off, although the city and state where the ceremony took place are included. Announcements usually take the form shown on the opposite page.

SAVE THE DATE CARDS

Another popular part of the wedding stationery these days are Save the Date cards. These simple cards, which can range from casual to formal, are sent to friends, family, and others who will be invited to the wedding, to let them know when and where the event will take place. They should be prepared and sent shortly after the reception hall has been booked and confirmed.

Mr. and Mrs. Robert L. Gibson
have the honour to announce
the marriage of their daughter
Kelly Jane
to
Mr. Mark John Barker
on Tuesday, the second of June
Nineteen hundred and seventy-seven
Council Bluffs, Iowa

ADDRESSING THE INVITATIONS AND ANNOUNCEMENTS

Printed or engraved invitations and announcements usually come in two envelopes and often come with tissue to protect the printing. I say usually because the custom is not hard and fast, and using one envelope and omitting the tissue does save trees. The custom of two envelopes dates back to Roman times, when correspondence was carried by messenger and the outer envelope was sealed to keep it from prying eyes. The tissue arose from the days when engraving was a far messier business than it is today, and something was needed to prevent the type from smearing. In a sense both are an affectation today, but more importantly, they are unnecessary. It is, I hasten to add, entirely

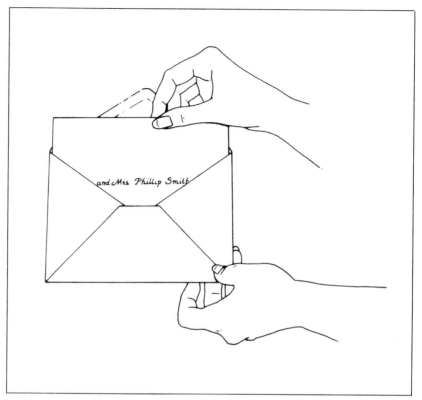

Correct way to enclose the double envelope

correct to send formal wedding invitations with or without the second envelope and with or without the tissue.

The inner envelope, which is ungummed, is placed inside the larger envelope so that the writing faces the flap. If the tissue is included, it should be placed over the printed or engraved part of the invitation.

The envelopes should be addressed on a day when your handwriting is at a peak—or perhaps someone in your family or a close friend with particularly lovely handwriting would be willing to address them for you. For a fee, as noted, you can also hire a professional calligrapher to address them for you. Only black or dark blue ink should be used. Abbreviations should not be used, except for *Mr.* and *Mrs.*

If an envelope is sent to a husband and wife, it should read:

Mr. and Mrs. Bruce James Stewart
522 South Tremont Street
Trenton, New Jersey 08608

The inner envelope repeats the name only:

Mr. and Mrs. Stewart

An invitation should never be addressed to *Mr. J. Johnson and wife,* nor should it say, *and family.* If you want to include children under eighteen in the invitation, on the inner envelope, write:

Mr. and Mrs. Stewart
Nancy, Amy, Rodney

Dates or fiancés of single guests, roommates, children over eighteen, and children living apart from their parents may be included on an invitation.

When you want someone to know he or she is free to bring a date, address the envelope:

Miss Karen Johnson and guest

Whenever you know someone's name, it should be included on the invitation. An engaged couple may be invited with one invitation, as may roommates:

Miss Carly Lord
Mr. Jack Jones

Or:

Mr. Harold Lee
Mr. Simon Masters

When children live with their parents, they can be included on the parents' invitation. When they live on their own, they are usually (but not always) sent separate invitations, which are addressed:

Misses Julie and Amy Steward

Or:

Messrs. Howard and Nathan Hall

An invitation sent to two people living together should read:

Miss Janet Bloom (or:) *Ms. Janet Bloom*
Mr. James Rodney

Or alternately:

Janet Bloom
James Rodney

The same format can be used for a married couple with two surnames. A widow is addressed as:

Mrs. John Flint Brown

Or:

Mrs. Mary Brown

A divorced woman is usually addressed as:

Mrs. Mary Brown

Or more formally, combining her maiden and married surnames:

Mrs. Flint Brown

A return address should be included on the envelope. It can be written on the back flap or the upper-left-hand corner of the envelope. The engraver can also engrave it in raised letters with no ink on the back flap.

A nice touch to any wedding invitation or announcement is to use a pretty, decorative postage stamp on the envelope. Check your post office to see what is available. When you buy the stamps, you might also have an invitation weighed, just to be sure it will go through the mails with the regular postage. Occasionally, elaborate invitations on heavy paper require extra postage—a source of embarrassment to the bride who didn't check first.

ORGANIZING YOUR RESPONSES

When you mail your invitations, set up a card file of the guests' names and addresses so you are ready to record their replies and keep a record of their gifts as they come in. The best way to do this is with note cards and a file box. Make out a 3-x-5-inch card for each guest and file it alphabetically. As the guests reply to the wedding, note their acceptance or regrets on their cards. A different color ink for each is especially helpful. When a gift arrives, pull out the card of the guest who sent it and note in detail what the gift is and the store from which it was sent, in case you find you must return it. As you write a thank-you note, make a notation on the card, along with the date the note was written. Whatever you do, don't leave this organization to the last minute, or you may never know who sent what gift and who has responded to your invitation.

10
Special Circumstances

MORE and more marriages these days involve some kind of special circumstances—a divorce in either the bride's or groom's family, a previous marriage on either the bride's or groom's part, a pre-wedding pregnancy, an intermarriage, and possibly the disapproval of one or both sets of parents. Such weddings are hardly impossible to carry off, but they do raise some issues of protocol. Who gives away the bride if her own father is not living? How are unfriendly, divorced parents seated at a wedding? How are remarried, divorced parents seated? What kind of wedding is appropriate for a pregnant bride? An older bride? This chapter attempts to answer all your difficult questions.

DIVORCE IN THE FAMILY

Many families today have been touched by divorce, and it can throw a monkey wrench into wedding plans. Although there are a few rules to follow, which I'll discuss below, the most important thing to remember is that people's feelings matter more than any rules. And this goes two ways: while a bride may well want her parents to behave in a certain way on her wedding day, she must accept that they may not be willing or able to do so. And in turn divorced parents of a child getting married should make every effort to bury any bad feelings they may have, because this is the most special day of their child's life.

A bride (or for that matter, a groom, although the wedding will be far less affected if his parents are divorced) should talk to both parents about the situation, sounding them out about what is possible and what is not. Many children, for example, long to have a wedding picture taken with both parents, even though they may have been divorced for years. This is the kind of thing to discuss in advance rather than waiting until your wedding day. The bride should be aware of hurt feelings that can arise, for example, when her parents are photographed with her and their current spouses are left out. A tactful bride will also arrange for pictures to be taken of her parents with her and their current spouses.

Who Gives the Wedding

If the bride's father has remained involved with his daughter and is willing to do so, he may pay for all or part of the wedding. If he does, he is treated as the official host, with the bride's mother acting as hostess. Their duties and seating arrangements, however, are organized so they need not stand together in the receiving line, nor need they sit together at the reception.

If the mother pays for the wedding, she alone acts as hostess (sometimes with the bride's stepfather), and the father is treated like an honored guest.

Divorced parents giving the wedding jointly can issue joint invitations (see the sample in chapter 9). It would not make for the clearest invitation, but I could even foresee a situation where, when both parents have remarried and all are on friendly terms, the invitation might be issued in all their names:

Mr. and Mrs. William Bosworth
and
Mr. and Mrs. Donald Walsh
request the honour of your presence
at the wedding
of
Mr. Bosworth's and Mrs. Walsh's daughter

. . .

Who Gives the Bride Away

This is perhaps the touchiest question a bride of divorced parents must answer. When the bride has remained close to her father and he is paying for the wedding, the answer is obvious: he escorts her. Her stepfather is, of course, an honored guest.

Generally, a birth father takes precedence over any other man in his right to escort his daughter down the aisle, provided he has remained a part of her life. But I've seen situations where the bride was reared and supported by her stepfather, and wanted him to give her away even though her real father would be present at the wedding. In such a case, after thoughtful examination of her feelings, she is entitled to be escorted by whoever makes her most comfortable.

I encourage parents to avoid putting any pressure on their children when they are making such emotional decisions. I greatly admired a stepfather I know for his selfless handling of this delicate situation when it arose in his family. He had reared a lovely young woman from the age of five, and then he stood by as her mostly absent father came back into her adult life shortly before her marriage. Seeing that his stepdaughter was flattered by her father's attentions and feeling pulled in two directions, he graciously told her he wanted to be with her mother on the special day, and thought it only fitting that her father escort her down the aisle.

I attended another wedding where stepfamilies were involved. The bride's father escorted her down the aisle, but when the minister asked who gave her in marriage, four people—her stepparents and her parents—seated across from each other in the front pews, responded, "We do."

Seating at the Wedding

If they have not remarried and have remained friendly, divorced parents may sit together at their child's wedding ceremony. If they are not friendly or have remarried, they sit separately or with their respective spouses, the mother in the first pew on the left (the bride's side) and the father one or two pews behind her. Once or twice I have seen parents and stepparents sit together. (You will know whether your stepparents get along well enough to sit close to one another, and should make your plans accordingly.)

If the bride's mother has not remarried, she usually asks her brother or some man to whom she is close to sit with her in her pew. An uncle or brother who gives a bride away always joins her mother in the first pew, and his wife sits with other relatives for the ceremony, rejoining her husband at the reception. If the mother has an escort, even though she may not have been seeing the man very long, she may feel that she wants to ask him to sit with her, and this is entirely proper. She does not, however, assign him to any other official role in the wedding.

Seating arrangements are similar for the groom's parents if they are divorced.

If parents are separated but not yet divorced, arrangements will simply have to be based on how they feel about each other. They may sit together or not.

At the Reception

Fathers often do not stand in the receiving line, so there is no reason for divorced parents to stand together. If the father is paying for the wedding or sharing the expenses, he circulates as any host would.

The best solution for seating is to put divorced parents at separate tables, each with their spouses and some of their relatives or close friends. By the way, no matter how poor relations are with a stepparent, he or she must be invited to the wedding. Not to do so is rude and forces the natural parent to make a very difficult decision about whether or not to attend anyway.

Sometimes when feelings between divorced parents are acrimonious, a father may attend the ceremony and give his daughter away, but elect, with her permission, not to attend the reception. He often holds another reception or wedding party for her at a later time to which he invites his friends and family, some of whom will also have attended the reception her mother gave. Those who have given gifts are not obligated to do so again. If the reception is held immediately after the mother's, the bride and groom may attend still wearing their wedding clothes. More often, though, the party is held on another day. The bride and groom dress in keeping with the formality of the day, but usually do not wear their wedding clothes.

DIVORCED OR WIDOWED BRIDE

Until a few years ago, it was socially taboo for a woman who had been married before to wear white or have a large wedding. While most brides who are remarrying do not want to wear a traditional wedding dress, many opt to wear white. Sometimes, too, they go ahead and have a large reception, mostly because they did not have one the first time around or because they have an entirely new set of friends who wish them well and want to celebrate their marriage.

Strictly speaking, guests are not obligated to send a gift to a wedding in which the woman has been married before, but in practice most persons are delighted to give their remarrying friends something for their new home.

The couple may even register their gift preferences, although they often skip this for a remarriage, or, at most, make their preferences known informally among their friends when they are asked. A second-time bride cannot expect her family and friends to outfit her with a household as they did the first time she married, since she presumably kept the belongings from the first marriage. In other words, it is better to register for a lovely bowl than for pots and pans, for a beautiful afghan than for blankets and sheets, although you may, when asked, tell a friend if you do need these practical things.

Perhaps because it is assumed that a divorced woman has kept her household belongings, and because every woman is believed to be entitled to one large wedding even if she marries a man who has been married before, the same restrictions do not apply to men who are remarrying. A man who is marrying for the second, third, or even the fifth time, to a woman who has never been married, can have as formal and large a wedding as his bride wants.

OLDER BRIDE

I'm pleased to report that the distinctions that used to be made for "older" brides—nothing white or bridish after thirty or thirty-five—no longer apply. Because so many women are marrying late, it is now not unusual to find an older bride who wants a traditional wedding, complete with a long wedding dress and veil.

It is, I feel, up to each individual woman's taste to draw the line regarding her age and her status as a bride. A certain kind of traditional wedding dress and veil is in a sense the province of the very young, but this is not to suggest that a woman of any age should not wear a white dress and veil to her wedding. Once she has passed a certain age, however, and only she knows what is comfortable for her, the white dress might be sophisticated and the veil might be a chic cocktail hat.

WHEN YOU'RE PREGNANT

If your pregnancy does not show and time permits, you may have any kind of wedding you want. It is inappropriate, though, for an obviously pregnant bride to wear a traditional wedding dress and have a large wedding. Your wedding should be intimate and informal.

WHEN YOU'RE COHABITING

Many couples today live together for several months to several years before they decide to tie the knot publicly. I've seen cohabiting couples have large weddings and receptions as well as modest ones. I've seen them have a fancy reception, or hold a simpler reception in their home. I personally think some discretion is in order. A couple who has cohabited for years probably should opt for a somewhat quiet wedding without all the fanfare, and unless everyone in their families knows they cohabit and no one disapproves, it is less touchy to hold the reception some place other than your shared home. Mostly I recommend maintaining this small degree of decorum so as not to offend old-fashioned great-aunts and grandparents. If you don't have any of these, and your parents have been visiting you as a couple for a long time without any problems, then you can have the reception in your home if you choose to.

INTERMARRIAGE

A religious intermarriage occasionally presents some special difficulties, despite the fact that so many couples are intermarrying. The Catholic church, for example, used to permit such weddings only when the non-Catholic partner signed papers promising to rear the children as Catholics. Today a non-Catholic marrying a Catholic may be required to undergo several meetings with a priest or take a brief class, but the couple will be permitted to marry in a Catholic Church.

Jews who intermarry with gentiles and want a Jewish ceremony will have more difficulty, as only a few rabbis are willing to officiate at such a wedding.

Occasionally clergypersons of different denominations will join together for a mixed-marriage ceremony. Usually the ceremony is performed in one religion, and prayers are offered by the assisting clergyperson.

If a religious ceremony is important to you, I urge you to keep looking until you find a clergyperson who will marry you in the kind of ceremony you want.

OPPOSITION TO YOUR MARRIAGE

Saddest and most difficult is when one or both sets of parents oppose your marriage. Actually, except where very young persons are involved, I think parents make a serious mistake in letting their feelings of dislike show toward their child's choice of a spouse. This kind of disapproval cuts deep and often causes a rift that never completely heals.

Before you begin to plan your wedding, try to resolve any differences, perhaps through a neutral, respected person who can talk to all parties.

If your parents oppose the marriage but are still willing to give you a wedding and will happily appear at the celebration, you can go ahead with your plans. If their opposition is bitter to the point where they will not attend the wedding, then you have no choice but to plan the wedding on your own. Most couples in this awkward situation opt for a small or informal wedding rather than a large social affair. Regardless of how small your wedding is, your parents should be given an opportunity to attend should their feelings change at the last moment.

Many couples, faced with what they view as insurmountable parental opposition, choose to elope, and this is of course a time-honored option. But if you do this, I hope for your own sakes that you will make the occasion a festive one. A marriage is too important not to celebrate. You might try to find a clergyperson or judge whom you know or have some connection with to marry you, rather than marrying at city hall. Take along some good friends, if possible, and be sure to plan a wedding celebration afterward—perhaps a breakfast or luncheon at your favorite restaurant.

DEATH OF A PARENT

If the bride's father is not living, she usually asks someone else to escort her down the aisle and act as host at her wedding. Since these need not be the same person, she has a chance to pass around the honors, if she wishes. A brother, usually older, grandfather, uncle—anyone, actually, who has acted as a father figure to her—may fill in. I've not seen this done, as I noted earlier, but if the bride has been reared by her mother and desires to do so, I would see nothing amiss in her mother escorting her down the aisle.

At the part in the ceremony when the clergyperson asks who gives the bride in marriage, her mother, sitting in the first pew, responds, "I do," or less often, the man who escorted the bride might respond, "Her mother and I do."

If a bride's mother is not living, she can ask an aunt or other close relative to act as her hostess.

Since no comparable roles to host and hostess exist for the groom's parents, he need not officially ask someone to substitute, but he, too, has an opportunity to honor some person who has acted as a parent to him by asking them to act as an unofficial host or hostess. Finally, a note to all family members involved with a wedding:

A wedding is for the bride and groom. It is their very special day. As such, it is a time to set aside family differences and behave as pleasantly to one another as you possibly can. Just as the tactful bride and groom must take into account their estranged parents' feelings, parents should make every effort to make this a time to be especially considerate of their children's emotional needs.

11
Organizing the Reception

THE minute you know you are getting married is the time to start planning your reception, particularly if the wedding and reception are going to be large. In every community, it seems there is one baker who does the loveliest wedding cakes or a florist who seems to specialize in the type of flower arrangements you like, and if you want to be sure of obtaining the services of these people, don't waste any time contacting them once you know you are going to be married.

Almost all the services required at a reception can be provided by specialists, or you can have a do-it-yourself reception as described in chapter 12.

THE FIRST STEP

Once you've lined up your attendants and drawn up a guest list, you should have a pretty good idea of the number of people who will be present at the rehearsal dinner, wedding, and reception.

Draw up a list of all the services you think you will need at your reception. Basically you will need a place in which to hold it, a florist, a baker to supply your wedding cake and any other baked goods you may choose, a photographer, musicians or some facilities for music, possibly a caterer to provide food, and possibly a supplier of liquor or champagne, depending upon the place you select for your reception and the services it offers.

Before you buy anything, contact as many suppliers as possible for general estimates and a rundown on their services. Tell them what you have in mind and try to be open to any suggestions they make. Ask about package deals and tipping policies. For a set price per person, some restaurants will provide everything from finger sandwiches to a seven-course meal. Other restaurants or catering services will charge for everything from the number of waiters required to each bottle of liquor consumed.

Once you have found a place that offers the services you need at a price you can afford, make an appointment to see the person in charge. Take in your detailed list and discuss everything you will need. Be sure to obtain a written estimate of costs and ask about penalties in case the reception must be canceled; this is your only protection against unnecessary costs. Reserve the room or rooms, and food, liquor, and other services you need as soon as possible. Specify, in writing, the exact services you want—cloth rather than paper tablecloths and napkins, glass rather than plastic glasses, no coat racks in sight, all signs off walls, plumbing and pipes covered with screens or drapes, tablecloths to cover the bar table, good china and silverware, all chairs in good condition, and so on.

THE FLORIST

The florist, too, should be lined up as early as possible. Careful thought should be given to the selection of a florist; if possible, find one who specializes in weddings. Or better yet, ask friends for the names of florists they have used, especially if you have seen someone's work and loved it.

Flowers are traditionally carried by the bride and her attendants, and worn as boutonnieres by the groom, his attendants, and the father of the bride. The mothers and grandmothers of the bride and groom are usually given corsages. The bride and her attendants may also wear flowers in their hair.

Flowers may also be placed on the altar, or used to mark off the church pews. Jewish couples are married under a *chuppah,* a canopy symbolizing their future home, and flowers are frequently used to decorate it. Some *chuppahs* are constructed entirely of flowers. When selecting flowers for the ceremony, remember that you are the focal point of the service and keep them simple enough so they don't detract from the event.

If you are being married at home, in a club or a hotel, flowers will be especially important, as they can form a backdrop replacing a church altar and can be used to mark off aisles. Flowers banked against a fireplace, bay window, or wall between two windows especially

Flowers banked against a window make a lovely setting for a home wedding.

contribute toward a lovely setting. Aisles can be created with standing urns filled with greenery and a few flowers tied with ribbon. For an evening wedding, flowers are often used with ribbons and candles. An arbor or archway constructed with greens and flowers makes an especially nice focal point at a garden wedding.

You will also need flowers for your reception. A bouquet will be needed for the service table, and one for the bride's table. If you are having a formal dinner, you may want floral arrangements at each table. Be sure table arrangements are low, so people can talk across the table.

The Number and Season of Flowers

Flowers can become a major cost at a wedding if you use great quantities of them. Remember that many lovely effects can be created with greenery and a small number of flowers.

Another way to eliminate unnecessary expense is to choose flowers that are in season, and a thoughtful florist will point out which these are. Generally, Easter lilies are traditional in early spring. White tulips and lilac are also lovely and in season for a spring wedding. White peonies are frequently used in May, and roses throughout the summer. Even daisies, simple as they are, form a charming bouquet combined with lacy ferns and baby's breath. White chrysanthemums are a lovely fall and winter flower. Careful thought should be given to the selection of flowers, for they add much to the beauty and romance of the ceremony.

Once you have selected a florist make an appointment to meet with him to discuss your overall needs. Ideally, meet with him at the reception site and at the place where your wedding will be held.

The florist will have one or more books showing flower arrangements, and he will also be able to supply you with countless suggestions. Making weddings beautiful is his business.

Flowers for You and the Bridesmaids

Most bridal bouquets are white or pastel. Some brides choose to have their bouquets made of silk flowers, which they can use later in their homes. Dried flower arrangements have also become popular. Some brides carry only one flower or a few flowers with a prayer book, but as a rule, the bride's bouquet is the most elaborate in the wedding party.

The flowers carried by you and your attendants should be coordinated in mood and color, and the maid of honor may carry different flowers from the bridesmaids. The fabric and style of dresses and the theme of the wedding should be taken into account when planning the flowers. An old-fashioned garden bouquet, for example, is lovely for a summer wedding where the bride and attendants are wearing organdy, but it is out of place at a formal wedding when everyone is wearing moiré or another formal fabric. Keep the bouquets fairly small. They should enhance, not overpower, the wedding party.

Flower girls carry a small basket of flowers or rose petals to strew about the church, or a nosegay. If you plan to have the flower girl scatter rose petals, check to be sure the church doesn't have rules against this.

Mothers and grandmothers always appreciate flowers that indicate their special status. They can be corsages or flowers to pin on their purses. Cymbidium orchids and roses are good choices; other traditional flowers include gardenias, violets, daisies, or a mixed flower arrangement.

Frequently the bride wears a corsage with her going-away outfit. If you want to do this, you can have it built into your bouquet so you can remove it just before you toss the bouquet.

Flowers for the Groom and His Attendants

The groom and every man in the wedding party—including both fathers—wear boutonnieres in their left lapels. The groom's boutonniere is frequently taken from the bride's bouquet—a single white rose, a sprig of stephanotis, or a sprig of lily of the valley. White carnations are the most popular flower for boutonnieres for the men. The ring bearer should be given a boutonniere to wear as well, and grandfathers also appreciate them.

Flowers for the Reception

Aside from the flowers you and your attendants carry, the most important and noticed flowers will be those at your reception. Tell the florist you want a masterpiece. Flowers are not necessary at either end of the receiving line, but banks of ferns or potted palms are a nice touch. Remember, too, that potted plants can be used to hide any minor eyesore in the room where the reception is held. You may also want a few banks of ferns or potted palms at the spot where you plan to take formal pictures.

If you have planned a formal dinner or a seated buffet, consider small centerpieces of a few flowers attached to a candle or a candelabrum flowing with greenery, ribbons, and a few flowers.

The bride and her attendants may arrange their bouquets on the bride's table to make the centerpiece.

A small nosegay is often used to top the wedding cake. If you plan to do this, remember to tell the baker to insert a small water container about the size of a shot glass on the top of the cake. The nosegay is placed in it after the cake is assembled, usually right before the reception. Greenery and rose petals are sometimes scattered on the tablecloth around the cake, and the bride's bouquet should be placed in plain view on the table while photographs of the cake-cutting are taken.

Other Services a Florist Offers

Florists who are wedding specialists will be able to supply a kneeling cushion for the bride and groom, a canvas runner for the aisle, standards for large flower arrangements at the altar or reception, candleholders and candles, white satin ribbon to rope off the front pews, a canopy between the sidewalk and the church door, a cushion for the ring bearer, and a special bouquet to be presented at the foot of the statue of the Blessed Virgin Mary—a tradition at Roman Catholic Weddings.

What the Florist Needs to Know

Aside from the obvious and already mentioned things, such as the theme of your wedding, a description of your dress and veil, and your attendants' dresses, the florist needs to know when and where to deliver the flowers. This may seem a minor point, but many a wedding has been delayed because of confusion over the arrival of flowers. Safest and most convenient is to have flowers for you and your attendants delivered to the church about two hours ahead of the service. The florist will usually show up to help the bride, bridesmaids, and flower girls with their flowers and to instruct them on just how to carry them. If he doesn't, remember that flowers should always be carried in their most natural position, that is, with the stems down. If a bride's bouquet is full at one end and tapers on the other, the tapered end is the bottom of the bouquet.

Flowers for mothers, grandmothers, and other honored guests are usually delivered to their homes, usually early on the day of the wedding, but they may also be sent directly to the wedding.

A form that can be copied and given to the florist to supply him with the information he needs to plan lovely and appropriate floral arrangements for your wedding and reception is on pages 209–210 of the Bride's Organizer.

As a final note, if you use a lot of floral arrangements at your wedding, put someone in charge of dispensing with them after the reception. You may want to give them to close friends who helped you with the wedding, or attendants, or send them to an old people's home or to some charitable organization. Hospitals rarely accept cut flowers anymore, but it is nice to offer them to someone who will appreciate their fleeting beauty.

THE BAKER

Wedding cakes are traditionally tiered and frosted in white, sometimes with some pastel touches. They are made of white cake, but brides who have other preferences are following up on them more and more often these days. It's not unusual these days to eat chocolate, carrot, or even, as I did recently, poppy seed wedding cake. The top tier of a wedding cake is often made of fruit cake that can be frozen and saved for future anniversaries.

You can choose either a professional baker or someone in your community who has built a reputation for making fabulous cakes—as long as it is someone with expertise in making wedding cakes. Many communities have a bakers' association that will refer you to one or more bakers. The women's page editor or food editor of your local newspaper may also be able to recommend someone.

Plan to meet with the baker to discuss your color and style preferences. Some bakers have sample books that you can use to select the cake. When you meet with the baker, have in mind the color theme of your wedding, the number of guests so the baker can determine the size of the cake, and any other baked items you may want, such as small pieces of cake that guests can take home with them.

The tradition of the tiny bride and groom atop the wedding cake seemed to be on the wane for a few years, but has now returned to popularity. Second choice for many brides is a small arrangement of flowers, and if this is your preference, be sure to so indicate to the baker so he can make appropriate arrangements.

Make arrangements for the cake to be delivered to the reception site several hours before the big event. Most multitiered wedding cakes are not brought to the reception already assembled, but need to be put together on the spot. Be sure to allow enough time between delivery and the reception to assemble the cake. The cake is usually placed on its own special table.

Some couples want small pieces of cake (either fruit or pound) in special souvenir boxes for the guests to take home. This is called groom's cake, and it is said that a single woman who places it under her pillow will dream of the man she will marry. The cake, which may be square, rectangular, triangular, or heart-shaped, is baked especially for this purpose and cut to the size of the box. The tiny white boxes may be plain or stamped with the name or initials of the bride and groom and the date of the wedding, and tied with ribbon. The boxes are arranged on a small table near where the guests exit. Some bakeries or caterers will prepare these all made up, or you can order the boxes and cake separately and assemble them at home. If you do not wish to go to the expense of supplying the boxes, do have a supply of cellophane bags ready for your guests to take their cakes home in. These individual cakes are expensive and are not often seen these days.

THE PHOTOGRAPHER

A phenomenon of the wedding day is that the bride and groom remember less about it than anyone else. Perhaps this is one reason that photographers have such an important role to play. Weddings truly are too beautiful to entrust to memory—and photographs will be especially treasured by everyone who is involved in the wedding.

Wedding photography is expensive. If you decide to save money by asking a friend to take pictures, be very sure that you will be happy with the results and that your friend and his or her camera are totally reliable. It is probably wisest, however, to engage a professional wedding photographer to record your special day.

Friends who have been recently married can suggest qualified persons, and you should talk with several photographers before you finally settle on one. Ask the photographers to supply references and check on them to be sure that you are hiring someone who is reliable. Meet with the photographers to look at their samples. Make sure that the photographer for your wedding will be the person whose samples you like. Ask for a written confirmation of price and the number of photographs in black and white and color that you are obligated to buy. Talk to the photographer about the kind of pictures you want and where you expect them to be taken to be sure that you both agree, so there will be no last-minute mix-ups or unmet expectations.

Basically, there are several kinds of photographs that you will want of your wedding: your official bridal portrait, formal portraits of you and the groom during the ceremony (if permissible), formal portraits of you and your wedding party and close members of your family, and candid pictures, usually taken during the reception.

Your Bridal Portrait

Your bridal portrait is taken either at the time of your last fitting or, occasionally, right before the ceremony. Many photographers come to the store to photograph you during your last fitting. If yours does, he or the store will probably supply some type of bouquet, but you might want to check on this in advance. Other photographers will prefer to photograph you in their studios, and some will come to your home, if that is preferred.

A bride's makeup is always best understated but well applied. Use your regular daytime makeup if a color portrait is taken, and perhaps slightly heavier makeup for a black-and-white portrait. The photographer can probably give you some advice on this, but you should stay with the makeup you are most comfortable wearing, so that your wedding portrait will look natural. For specific hints on looking your best for the bridal portrait, see chapter 14.

Photographs of the Wedding and Reception

Insist on the most unobtrusive, natural photography possible. Modern photographic equipment makes it possible to record your wedding and reception without the use of flashbulbs and from a distance, so that the ceremony is not disturbed and guests are rarely aware of the photographer's presence.

The videotaping of weddings is growing in popularity, if not in artfulness. I can understand that couples want to preserve their weddings in this fashion, but many of the videotapes I have seen are not skillfully done, consisting as they do of long, boring scenes of people going through the receiving line or dancing and eating. Even the custom of passing a microphone around to each guest so they can extend their best wishes to the bride and groom palls after the twentieth guest—with just one hundred more to go. One suggestion I can make is to work with the cameraperson and possibly even to give him or her a list of what you want shot. Use the same list as for the still photographer. Of course, the entire event can be videotaped and then edited down, but then you will be leaving some major decisions in the hands of the cameraperson.

Formal portraits of you and your wedding party, except for a few at the altar immediately after the ceremony, as well as family pictures, should be taken after everyone has gone through the receiving line. It is rude to keep guests waiting while you have your picture taken.

The "posed" pictures you will want as keepsakes will probably include:

- ☐ You and your groom
- ☐ You alone with your mother
- ☐ You alone with your father
- ☐ You with your mother and father together
- ☐ You with the groom's parents
- ☐ You with your attendants in a group and in individual pictures with each attendant
- ☐ The groom with his attendants
- ☐ The wedding party, usually at the altar
- ☐ You and the groom with grandparents and any favorite relatives or honored guests

Traditional pictures taken at the church include:

- ☐ Each attendant, including flower girl and ring bearer, as he or she waits to walk down the aisle (especially nice if you give these photographs as remembrances from you)
- ☐ Your mother coming down the aisle with an usher
- ☐ The groom's parents coming down the aisle with an usher
- ☐ Wedding party at altar
- ☐ You and the groom exchanging vows, exchanging rings, and kissing at end of ceremony

Some of the "candid" pictures you will want to capture include:

- ☐ You putting on your veil, perhaps with your mother's or a bridesmaid's assistance
- ☐ Informal shots of you and your attendants just before the ceremony
- ☐ Informal shots of you and your father leaving for the church
- ☐ Random shots of guests going through receiving line (Ask a

close friend to point out special persons to the photographer at this time.)
- [ ] "Formal" shots of the guests at their tables (This ensures that you will have a record of everyone who attended.)
- [ ] Your first dance with the groom, and dances with your father and father-in-law
- [ ] Cutting the cake and feeding it to each other
- [ ] Toasting each other
- [ ] Toasts offered to you by others
- [ ] Tossing the garter (Your groom removes it first. Be graceful about this and help him by moving it below your knee—this will also help to avoid the suggestion of "cheesecake" that comes when your wedding dress is pulled up around your thigh.)
- [ ] Tossing your bouquet
- [ ] Telling your parents good-bye after the reception
- [ ] You and the groom leaving in car

As a final reminder, be sure the photographer has the address and time of the wedding. Call him to remind him again of the exact time, a few days before the wedding.

THE MUSIC

Music probably provides more ambience than anything else at a reception. It sets the tone. It helps to control the flow of events. Slightly fast, happy music will probably make the receiving line move more quickly, and it will get the reception off to a dazzling start. Slow music is romantic, and no music can signal the end of the reception.

If you can afford it, it is a nice touch to hire musicians for this special occasion. A pianist or violinist is a good choice, since you need only one. Three to five musicians is ideal if you have dancing, and, of course, you can have a full dance orchestra if that is your choice. If you hire a band or an orchestra, be sure the contract has an "in-person" clause to ensure that you get the same musicians you heard in rehearsal and not substitutes.

The union requires that musicians play for a specified time and then take a break, so if possible, hire a musician to play during the break in order to maintain the festive mood.

You can have any kind of music you want—even rock music, although keep in mind that an extended period of loud music may drive away your older guests. Remember that weddings are romantic events. I think waltzes and other slow music mixed in with some fast numbers provide the maximum amount of fun for the most guests.

Less expensive than hiring a band or other live musicians is to hire a disc jockey who will play records or tapes. And if you're really on a budget, tape some of your favorite music, hook up a stereo, and use that.

There is a trend today for band leaders and disc jockeys to act as masters of ceremonies, which you may or may not want for your wedding. The advantage is that you don't have to worry about anything. He tells you when to throw your bouquet, when to cut the cake, and will even introduce your wedding party. The disadvantage is that what are intended to be spontaneous ceremonies often end up being overdone—and sometimes, poorly done. I've seen some gauche things, such as a band playing inappropriately risqué music while the usher who caught the garter put it on the leg of the person who caught the bouquet—and in this case, the bouquet was caught by an eleven-year-old girl. When you hire someone to handle the music, talk to them in advance about what else you want them to handle and how you want it carried out.

On page 215 of the Bride's Organizer, you'll find a form to help organize the music for your reception.

BEVERAGES FOR THE RECEPTION

The drinks you serve at your reception are a matter of your personal taste. Traditionally, brides and grooms toast each other with champagne, but the toasts can be made with punch, either alcoholic or nonalcoholic, mixed drinks, or wine. The cost of liquor will be a major part of the reception expense, so you will want to buy it carefully and wisely.

Regardless of how you are charged by the caterer or reception hall, you should estimate the amount of liquor or drinks that will be required. Estimating the number of drinks to be served will also help the caterer determine the number of people required to tend bar, the amount of mix to order, and the amount of glasses and ice to provide. Plan on three to four drinks per person over a three-hour period. One bartender will be needed for every fifty people served.

Even if the beverages are included with the cost of catering, you can still have something to say about what is served.

Champagne

The traditional wedding beverage is purchased by the fifth, or in even larger sizes. Call several liquor dealers to get estimates on the most economical purchase. Champagne glasses vary in size from three to six ounces.

Imported French champagne is the most expensive; domestic champagne costs considerably less. After you get your liquor merchant's advice on champagne, buy one or two bottles and try them yourselves, perhaps over quiet dinners. The variety in taste and dryness of champagnes makes it necessary for you to sample them to know where your preference lies.

Wines

You can make your selection from among thousands of wines, and you will probably want to follow the advice of a good wine merchant before you make your final selection. It is also a good idea to sample the wines you are considering.

Generally, white wines are served with white meat and red wines with red meat. Wines produced in Europe, and especially in France, are usually more expensive than domestic wines, but this can vary so talk to a good wine merchant. The year a wine is gathered is known as the vintage, and wine gathered during a good year is also more expensive than one gathered during a lesser year.

White wines are chilled, and red wines, which should also be opened and allowed to breathe for about two hours prior to serving, are served at a cool room temperature. If you decide to serve wines, ask a friend or bartender to be sure the wines are properly handled.

Liquor

You can serve a variety of mixed drinks or limit the choice to one or two. Whiskey sours, screwdrivers, and Bloody Marys are ideal for a brunch or early afternoon reception. Another advantage to serving a limited selection of drinks is that they can be served from punch bowls or pitchers.

In large quantities, liquor is most economically bought in quarts or half-gallons. If you are buying by the case, you can also buy by fifths. Twelve fifths make up a case. When buying cases of liquor, ask the dealer for a discount. At 1½ ounces per drink and three drinks per person, 1½ cases should serve 100 people. Buy whatever mix you will need for punch or mixed drinks, and plan to have some extra around for children and people who don't drink alcoholic beverages.

On pages 216–217 of the Bride's Organizer is a form to help you choose and order the right amount of beverages for the reception.

OTHER ACCESSORIES FOR THE RECEPTION

An assortment of paper accessories also may be needed at a reception. Be sure to order matches, paper napkins, place cards, and cake boxes if needed. These items are usually printed with the names or initials of the bride and groom and the date of the wedding. Gold or silver ink are traditional, but you can select any color you like. Anything that requires printing should be ordered at least eight weeks before the reception.

CHOOSING A HOSPITALITY COMMITTEE

Receptions are for people. Too often a bride becomes so carried away with her starring role that she forgets that everyone at the wedding is her guest. Remember that you and your groom should circulate among the guests, thanking them for coming and making sure that they are having a good time.

Often the most awkward moments at a wedding reception are the early ones, when the wedding party may be off having their pictures taken or when some people are going through the receiving line while others are merely waiting before or after going through it. An excellent way to ease these awkward moments is to ask several friends or couples to serve as your hospitality committee. To determine how to station your friends so they can be most useful, go to the place of your reception and map out a floor plan showing where you will put the buffet tables, receiving lines, cake and refreshment table, and guest book. This will make it easy to station your hospitality committee where it can be most helpful.

If the reception is large, you will want to ask friends to serve in shifts. Call or write brief notes asking people if they will pay you the honor of assisting at your wedding. Tell each one exactly what his or her duties will be and when he or she will be needed. Having definite plans and duties for all assistants ensures that your reception will go as smoothly as possible, whether it is held at home or elsewhere.

A sample note from your mother outlining a helper's responsibilities might read:

Dear Mary Lou and Bob,

Thank you for your kindness in offering to assist at Bob and Jackie's reception Friday, the 16th of May. Jackie and I would like you to take charge of the guest book from 4 to 5 o'clock. I hope this time meets with your approval. If not, please let me know so that we can make any necessary changes. Janet Young will be in charge of the assistants' list at the reception, so you may want to seek her out when you arrive. We are looking forward to seeing you and, again, thank you very much.

Affectionately,
Jane Stewart [bride's mother]

A bride could also write such a note. After the reception, be sure to write thank-you notes to each person who helped.

Among the duties you might wish to delegate are the following:

1. Taking charge of the bridal guest book
2. Passing champagne, lemonade, cold water to waiting receiving line (Be sure there is a table nearby to put glasses on before guests go through the line.)
3. Cutting and serving the wedding cake
4. Pouring and serving the coffee, punch, or tea at buffet table
5. Taking charge of the bridal gift book and table, including gift cards
6. Passing sandwiches, canapés, mints, and other food
7. Keeping the buffet tables and plates filled
8. Assisting in the kitchen if kitchen help is limited
9. Greeting guests at each door or entrance to the home or garden, or outside near the reception room at public halls in hotels
10. Showing guests where to hang coats
11. Inviting guests to see the wedding gifts

12. Assisting with decorations, the night before or the day of wedding
13. Passing the rice or paper rose petal bags
14. Circulating among the guests, introducing themselves and introducing others
15. Passing the boxed pieces of wedding cake
16. Removing empty plates and cups after the guests have been served
17. Introducing the bride's mother to any guest she might not know
18. Taking care of the groom's parents, introducing them, and serving them

12

A Do-It-Yourself Reception

FEW receptions are more special or meaningful than one you do yourself. That such receptions are also often held in the bride's parents' home only adds to their specialness. A reception that you plan yourself inevitably bears your own personal stamp—and for a woman with a strong sense of individuality and creativity, this is another bonus to a do-it-yourself reception. This kind of reception does require many extra hours of work, and it isn't something you should tackle alone. Fortunately, people love to help with weddings, and you will have little trouble enlisting whatever aid you need.

THE FIRST STEP

If the wedding and reception will take place in your home, the first thing you should do is plan where you want the ceremony to take place. Then figure out where you want the main activities of the reception—cutting the cake, toasting—to occur. Draw up lists of everything you will need—tables, flowers or plants for a backdrop for the ceremony, serving pieces, a coat rack, extra chairs. Many of these things, including silverware and dishes, can be rented for the day or borrowed from friends.

Plan the menu. Unless the wedding is very small, most do-it-yourself receptions are casual buffets. Small sandwiches and punch are ideal, although you can also serve a more substantial buffet of ham or roast beef and side dishes, along with mixed drinks.

Even if you are handling everything yourself, you might want to allow yourself one luxury. Hire a bartender and one or two persons to serve and pass the food. The bride doesn't serve the food at her reception, even if she has prepared it all, and the use of a few people to take over this task will add a professional, elegant note.

THE WEDDING CAKE

If you decide to make your own wedding cake, the "recipe" that follows is excellent and can be done with a minimum of effort.

6 *frozen vanilla layer cakes (17 ounces each)*

1 *16½-ounce can vanilla frosting or your favorite homemade white frosting*

Wedding ornament or flowers for the top

Arrange four cakes in a large square on a serving platter. Stack the remaining two cakes on top of each other to form the second layer. The already frosted cakes need only a light touch-up with frosting to join the seams. Canned frosting and a pastry tube can add the finishing touches of fancy trims. Position a decoration or flowers on the top of the cake. This cake serves 40.

Other recipes are available for the traditional round, multitiered wedding cake.

When you serve the cake, keep a damp cloth handy so you can clean the knife from time to time. Before you begin cutting, remove the top tier. You may want to freeze it and save it for a special occasion such as your first anniversary. Next cut a circle about two inches in from the outer edge. Working from this circle out, make vertical cuts about an inch apart until the entire ring is sliced into wedge-shaped pieces. Remove these pieces of cake to individual serving dishes. Cut another circle two inches from the edge and repeat the above procedure, which will leave a core of cake when the tier is finished. When you have cut one tier, begin to cut the next tier in the same way. The chart shows the number of people served by each size tier of cake.

SIZE OF TIER (ROUND)	NUMBER OF SERVINGS
6 inches	16
8 "	30
10 "	48
12 "	68
14 "	92
16 "	118
18 "	148

MAKING YOUR OWN PUNCH

To please everyone, you may want to serve a nonalcoholic and an alcoholic punch. The following recipes are excellent. To open champagne, hold the bottle in one hand and turn the cork with your other

Correct way to cut a tiered wedding cake

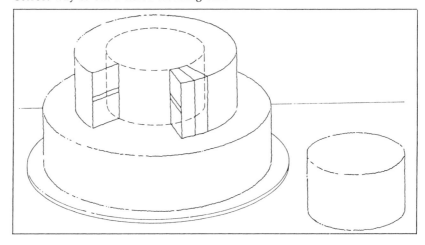

hand. Be sure to hold the bottle pointing away from your face. Gradually work the cork out.

Nonalcoholic Wedding Punch

4 *cups sugar*

4 *cups water*

2 *cups strong black tea*

6 *6-ounce cans frozen lemonade concentrate, undiluted*

2 *6-ounce cans frozen orange juice concentrate, undiluted*

2 *46-ounce cans pineapple juice (5 cups)*

2 *cups cut-up fresh strawberries and juice (or 16 ounces frozen strawberries, thawed)*

1 *gallon water*

2 *quarts dry ginger ale*

Make syrup by boiling sugar and 4 cups of water for ten minutes. Add tea and fruit juices. Chill two to three hours. Add remaining ingredients. Pour over block of ice in punch bowl or over ice cubes. Makes 60 to 70 servings.

Champagne Wedding Punch

10 *fifth bottles brut champagne*

¾ *cup cognac*

¾ *cup yellow Chartreuse*

¾ *cup Cointreau*

3 *fifths sparkling water*

Sugar to taste

Slices of fresh orange, lemon, and pineapple

Fresh mint

Mix all the liquids, adding sugar to taste. Set a ring of ice in a punch bowl and pour in the mixture. Garnish with the fruit slices and mint sprigs. Makes about 70 servings.

Champagne Peach Punch

2 *12-ounce cans peach nectar*

1 *6-ounce can frozen orange juice concentrate, undiluted*

3 *cups water*

¼ *cup lemon juice*

⅛ *teaspoon salt*

3 *large bottles California champagne, well chilled*

Combine all ingredients except champagne and chill well. At serving time, put in punch bowl over small chunk of ice or ice cubes. Add chilled champagne. Makes about 42 servings.

Champagne Orange Punch

2 *6-ounce cans frozen orange juice concentrate, undiluted*

1 *6-ounce can frozen lemonade concentrate, undiluted*

1½ *quarts ice water*

1   *large bottle California champagne*

    Orange slices

Dilute orange juice and lemonade concentrates with ice water in punch bowl. Just before serving, add well-chilled champagne and garnish with orange slices. Makes about 24 servings.

THE FOOD

The recipes that follow will each make enough sandwiches to serve 100 people. Simply cut down the quantity of food or increase it if you are serving fewer or more people, or if you want to have an assortment of foods.

Tea Sandwiches

8–10   *loaves thin-sliced bread (or 12–14 loaves regular-sliced bread)*

   3   *pounds butter or margarine*

   2   *quarts mayonnaise*

Fillings:

PINEAPPLE/HAM: Mix 4 pounds coarsely ground cooked ham, 4 pounds soft cream cheese, 4 1-pound, 4-ounce cans crushed pineapple, drained.

HAM SALAD: Mix 6 pounds coarsely ground cooked ham, 4 cups minced celery, 3 cups pickle relish, 4 cups mayonnaise, 4 tablespoons Worcestershire sauce.

HAM AND CHEESE: Mix 3 pounds coarsely ground cooked ham, 3 pounds coarsely grated cheddar cheese, 2 cups undiluted evaporated milk, 3 cups pickle relish, 4 teaspoons dry mustard, 2 teaspoons salt, ½ teaspoon pepper.

CHICKEN SALAD: Mix 16 cups diced, cooked chicken (6 4-pound stewing chickens or 4 32-ounce cans boned chicken), 6 cups diced celery, 4–6 cups mayonnaise.

TUNA SALAD: Substitute 16 6½- or 7-ounce cans tuna (16 cups) for chicken in chicken salad recipe above.

EGG SALAD: Substitute 80 chopped hard-cooked eggs for chicken in chicken salad recipe.

SLICED TURKEY, HAM, OR BEEF: Use 2 30-pound, or 4 18-pound turkeys (or a 12–16-pound ham, sliced, or roast beef, rolled rib, about 40–50 pounds).

CREAM CHEESE: Mix 8 pounds soft cream cheese with one of these: 4 pounds crumbled crisp bacon; 7 cups chopped stuffed olives; 4 cups chopped nuts.

SLICED MEAT: Hot or cold: To serve cold sandwiches, use 6 heads of lettuce and one of the following meats. To serve hot sandwiches, substitute 14 quarts of gravy for lettuce. Roast beef, rolled rib, weight (bone-in): 40–50 pounds.

SMOKED TONGUE: 40 pounds.

ROAST TURKEY: 2 30-pound birds.

Cut sandwiches into squares, diamonds, and rounds. They can be spread and assembled (borrow large trays from relatives and friends if necessary) the morning of the wedding, then covered and refrigerated until serving time. If this is your plan, make sure you have plenty of help. You don't want to be exhausted for your own wedding. It's a good idea to make whatever you can in advance.

ADDITIONAL TOUCHES

Mints and nuts add a delicious and relatively inexpensive touch to the reception. Four pounds of each should be adequate, along with sandwiches and a punch, for a reception of 100 guests.

If you serve liquor at the reception, it's always a good idea to provide coffee for your guests near the end of the reception. For 100 guests, you'll need about three pounds of coffee, one quart of cream, and one pound of sugar. Borrow or rent a large urn to serve it in.

You can use your imagination in planning the decorations. Such things as candles, greenery, and pretty tablecloths can be bought for very little or borrowed, and they can provide an atmosphere that makes the wedding especially memorable.

Although you can plan to hold the wedding outdoors, make contingency plans in case the weather does not cooperate. If you have the wedding outdoors, consider renting a large colorful tent to add to the atmosphere of gaiety.

13
Dressing for Your Wedding

YOU will soon discover that shopping for your wedding dress is not so simple as shopping for a new suit to wear to work.

For one thing, the type of dress and headpiece you choose depends upon the formality of your wedding. For another, wedding dresses are custom-ordered and fitted to you. As a rule, you can't go into a store and choose a wedding dress and walk out with it the same day. If you're really on a tight schedule, and you visit a bridal shop at the right time (when they're getting rid of one season's samples to make way for new ones), you may be able to buy a sample dress, but for a formal or semiformal wedding, it's better to plan very far ahead where your wedding dress is concerned.

CHOOSING YOUR DRESS

This means you should make an appointment as soon as possible with one or more bridal departments or stores to try on sample dresses. Bridal gowns are designed for two seasons: spring/summer and fall/winter. Spring/summer gowns arrive in the stores in December, and fall/winter gowns in May.

Anywhere from eight weeks to four or six months are required to make your gown, so choosing and ordering it should be one of your top priorities once you know you are getting married. Another reason to choose early is that the design of your dress will dictate what you will choose for your attendants. Until you select the colors for your wedding, your mother and mother-in-law cannot shop for their dresses, either.

When you make your appointment, tell the clerk your price range so you can be shown dresses you can afford, and, if you know, give the person some idea of the kind of dress you are looking for.

Sample dresses come in size 8. Once you have made your choice, you will be measured and your dress will be custom-made to fit you. Even if the sample fits you like a glove, insist that your measurements be taken. The sample may have stretched through repeated try-ons.

Expect to put down one-third of the total cost of the dress as a deposit. You should also ask for a written receipt—one that details

your measurements, the style of the dress, and the delivery date. Ask about cancellation fees. Most stores will not return your deposit, and a wedding dress order usually cannot be canceled. Some can be canceled if you call within a certain number of days, usually three to five.

Semiformal and formal wedding dresses cost between $180 and $400, although a designer dress or one made with expensive fabric can cost thousands. Headpieces cost from $40 to several hundred dollars.

Wedding dresses, as I'm sure you know, are traditionally white. What you may not know is that there are many shades of white, and that the same dress can often be ordered in white, ivory, or even a pink or blue tint.

If your skin has a yellow undertone, beige and ivory whites will flatter you. If it has a pink or bluish cast to it, you will look best in a pure white. But the only way to know for sure which shade of white or pastel flatters you is to try on dresses in various shades and tints until you find the one that makes you glow.

Wedding dresses are usually made of rich, luxurious fabrics, although I've seen several beautiful summer wedding dresses of cotton. You will pay more for a real fabric—real satin or taffeta, for example, instead of a polyester-blend satin or taffeta. Real lace is expensive, and antique lace adds even more to the cost of a dress.

Popular fabrics for winter/fall wedding dresses are lace, crepe, taffeta, moiré, peau de soie, brocade, and heavy silks. Lighter-weight spring/summer fabrics are organza, chiffon, lightweight silks, linen, eyelet, and dotted swiss—plus, as I mentioned, cotton. Beading and lace are used for summer and winter dresses, but they are usually heavier in the winter.

Wedding-dress designers, well aware of the fantasy element of what they create, often look to historical periods for inspiration, and should you want a dress that is "old-fashioned"—Victorian, Edwardian, Renaissance—you'll probably be able to find it.

At Your Fitting

When you try on wedding dresses, wear accessories similar to what you expect to wear with the dress. Obviously, if you buy a low-cut dress, you may have to buy a special bra, but it's a good idea to take one along if you already own it. Don't wear knee socks and running shoes. Wear shoes of the same heel height as you expect to wear on your wedding day. And wear the same amount of makeup that you expect to wear. Be sure your hair is styled, if possible, in a way similar to what you hope to do with it on your wedding day. All these factors will help you choose the dress that is most flattering to you.

When Your Budget Is Tight

If you're on a tight budget or getting married again and not looking for a traditional wedding dress, there are several possibilities. Sometimes you can buy a sample dress marked down. Or consider choosing a bridesmaid dress since they are less expensive than wedding dresses. Some bridesmaids' dresses can be ordered in white. Or look elsewhere than the bridal departments—in evening wear, for example.

When Your Wedding Is Small and Informal

You'll wear street clothes to a small, informal wedding, which means you can skip the bridal department and look elsewhere. Look at cocktail dresses or consider buying a stunning white suit, if you're the tailored type. If you want to splurge, go directly to a hat designer and order a custom-made hat to match your outfit. Often, you can use a hat to dress up a tailored suit or dress. Have it made of satin or add feathers or beads and attach a small veil. As a bride you won't want to wear much jewelry, so let yourself go all out on a great hat. It's a truly sophisticated touch.

An Heirloom Gown

Some brides are lucky enough to have a dress that has been handed down through the family, perhaps through a grandmother or greataunt. If such a gown is offered to you, and it suits your taste and looks

Bow

Juliette cap

Pillbox

Tiara

Wreath cap and puffy veil

marvelously flattering on you, by all means wear it. On the other hand, if you really don't like the dress or its style doesn't suit you well, graciously decline to wear it. Your choice of a wedding dress is highly personal, and you should not feel any pressure to wear one you aren't fond of. You can tactfully tell the well-meaning relative who offers the dress that you have always wanted your own wedding dress and have planned it to the most minute detail. If you decide to wear an heirloom dress, have it fitted to you if necessary.

CHOOSING YOUR HEADPIECE

Second in importance only to your gown is the headpiece you choose to set it off. Headpieces, like wedding dresses, vary in formality and are chosen to complement the dress. The one you pick should match exactly the shade of your dress and generally should be made of a similar or complementary material. If you know you want your headpiece made of matching fabric, ask the bridal consultant who takes your order to order an extra half-yard of fabric that matches your dress. If the store can't make your headpiece, it may be able to recommend someone who can do it. Some brides make their own headpieces. If you can sew or enlist the aid of a talented friend, you can design and sew your own headpiece and veil without too much trouble.

A headpiece should be chosen because it flatters you. Take your hair style, face shape, and figure into consideration. Of course, you will want to try on various headpieces with the dress you have chosen.

Tall, oval-faced women can wear almost any style of headpiece. Persons with round faces and short women may want to select a headpiece that adds height. A long face is softened by a band or wreath cap and a full, puffy veil. Tiaras are especially flattering to women who wear glasses or have round faces. The Juliet cap is particularly flattering to someone who is a little overweight or is short. It looks best worn with a short veil.

The romantic wide-brimmed hat is most becoming on a medium to tall woman with chin- or shoulder-length hair. It usually goes with an informal wedding dress or a suit or daytime dress, but it can be worn with certain stylish, long wedding dresses.

These style hints are not hard and fast rules. You may find that you look especially good in a mantilla even if you aren't tall and stately. Try on the various styles and choose the one that you love and look beautiful wearing.

Most headpieces come with a veil. The four-yard cathedral veil is generally worn only at a very formal wedding. This veil can replace a train on the dress or be worn with one. An elbow-length or finger-tip-length veil is the choice of most brides who want a formal look. It especially flatters a short-sleeved wedding dress and also shows off a pretty back. Bridal gowns made of clingy materials like jersey and dressy knits look wonderful with a cascade veil—an almost straight veil from a simple headpiece.

If you plan to dance at your wedding, you may want a veil that can be removed from the headpiece. Similarly, if your dress has a train, ask the store to sew buttons on the back of the dress so the train can be bustled when it's time to dance.

YOUR ACCESSORIES

You will probably want a new lacy set of lingerie to wear with your wedding dress. It should be white or a very pale pastel or beige and delicately detailed—the nicest you can afford.

Shoes are dyed to match and are usually chosen in a material that matches or coordinates with your wedding dress. Silk is appropriate with every fabric. Peau de soie or satin works well with winter fabrics. Linen is good for summer fabrics. You can wear a pump or a dressy sandal. Buy your shoes well in advance of your wedding day so you can "practice" walking in them and break them in.

A light coating of sand applied to the soles of your shoes on your wedding day is extra insurance against slipping as you walk down the aisle.

Gloves, which used to be *de rigueur* for any wedding, are now a matter of choice, and many brides choose not to wear them and do not ask their attendants to wear them, either. After all, not every wedding dress looks good with them. Many long-sleeved dresses are incompatible with gloves, for example. But many brides in short-sleeved dresses are rediscovering gloves as a fetching accessory.

If you wear kid gloves, which are traditional with formalwear, choose silk-lined ones that can be easily removed. If you wear long gloves, slit the glove along the third finger of your left hand so that your ring can be slipped on during the ceremony. If you wear short gloves, slip off one or both at the altar and hand them to your maid of honor. Alternately, fingerless lace gloves can be worn.

SAVING YOUR GOWN

You may want to have your dress preserved so it can be offered to a good friend or sister, or cut up to make a christening gown. A professional cleaner will be able to advise you on preserving your gown; the cost is about $65.

CHOOSING YOUR ATTENDANTS' DRESSES

Choose your attendants' outfits at the same time or shortly after your dress is selected. They, too, take at least eight weeks to order, and then fittings are usually required. On pages 204–207 of the Bride's Organizer you'll find forms to record the necessary measurements.

Attendants' dresses should be similar in style, mood, and fabric to your dress. They need not be the same fabric, but if your dress is peau de soie, you won't want your attendants wearing velvet. Also, if you are wearing a Victorian-style dress, you will want your attendants' dresses to match the mood.

Although your bridesmaids must accept your choice of a dress for them, you want each woman to be dressed in a style that is flattering to her, so take your attendants' figures and personalities into account when you choose their dresses. Also take their coloring into account when selecting colors.

If your bridesmaids have different colorings, consider choosing their dresses in various shades of your theme color, or consider dressing them in a rainbow of colors. That way, you can accommodate their individual colorings better. Occasionally, a bride chooses to dress her wedding party entirely in white; it can be stunning.

Your attendants will probably be paying for their own dresses, so also show consideration for cost when you choose their dresses. Remember that they will probably have to buy shoes and accessories, too. A small deposit is usually required when the dresses are ordered, and the full amount is paid after the final fitting.

The maid and/or matron of honor may wear a dress of a different shade or slightly different style than the other attendants. Or her bouquet can be slightly different from the others in shape or color.

If one is available, your flower girl can wear a dress that is a variation on the bridesmaids' dresses, but she can also wear any pretty dress in the wedding theme color.

ATTENDANTS' ACCESSORIES

Your attendants will also need to accessorize their dresses—something to keep in mind when considering expensive bridesmaids' dresses. You can choose shoes for your attendants, or you can tell them what style you want—plain pumps, sandals—and let them choose their own even if they do not exactly match. If the dresses are long, chances are no one will notice. If shoes must be dyed to match, then they all may as well be the same. And it's a good idea to have all the shoes dyed at the same place so they truly do match.

Attendants wear the headpiece you choose, and it should complement their dress—and their face shapes. If you want your attendants to wear jewelry—something such as pearl button earrings or a small pin—consider presenting the jewelry as your gifts to your bridesmaids. Otherwise, attendants should wear no jewelry, with the possible exception of earrings or a string of pearls.

YOUR JEWELRY

Traditionally a bride wears little jewelry—usually only an heirloom piece or something appropriate that the groom has given her. Pearls are always appropriate, as is gold. If you wear your engagement ring, remember to switch it to your right hand for the ceremony, or if your engagement ring is one that interlocks with the wedding band, give it to the groom before the ceremony. Watches are never worn by any member of the wedding party—this is a day when, symbolically, time does not matter. Bracelets are not usually worn by a bride, either.

YOUR TROUSSEAU

These days, most brides do not shop for a closetful of clothes, but you should fill in with anything you will need for your wedding trip or the parties preceeding your wedding. If you will be moving to another part of the country, buy whatever clothing you will need before you are married. Your clothing should also be suitable to your new life. Whether you will be a sophisticated urban wife who does a lot of entertaining or a career-oriented wife, plan your wardrobe accordingly.

WEDDING OUTFITS FOR THE MOTHERS

As soon as the bride has chosen her dress and decided on the theme color (or colors) for her wedding, the mothers can begin to shop for their dresses. The two mothers usually consult over the colors of their dresses to be sure they do not buy anything that clashes in photographs, and while they do not necessarily wear the wedding colors (although they may choose a shade or tint, if it is not exactly the same as the attendants' dresses), they do not want to clash with the wedding party, either. As a rule, the mothers of the bride and groom wear neither black nor white.

If the wedding is informal or held during the day, the mothers wear short dresses. They usually wear short evening or long dresses to a semiformal evening wedding, and long dresses to a formal evening wedding.

The later in the day the wedding is held, the dressier the mothers' gowns can be. Fortunately, the day of the costumey "mother-of-the-bride dress" is gone. Mothers may choose anything from an elegant wool dress to an elaborate and brightly colored evening gown.

THE GROOM AND HIS ATTENDANTS

What the men in the wedding party wear depends upon the formality of the wedding and the hour it is held. For the sake of uniformity, the men in the wedding party—the groom, the ushers, the best man, and the bride's father—usually rent their outfits, although occasionally, they wear their own.

The father of the groom should dress like the wedding party only if he will be standing in the receiving line. For a formal, evening wedding, he would wear white or black tie, and for a semiformal or informal wedding, he wears a business suit.

A small suit identical to the ones the adults are wearing can probably be rented for the ring bearer, or you can opt for a more traditional look: navy shorts and matching knee socks, a matching blazer, and white shirt and tie.

For a formal evening wedding, either white tie or black tie is worn, depending upon the preference of the bride and groom. White tie consists of a black tailcoat, satin-striped trouser, a wing-collar shirt, a white single-breasted waistcoat, and a white bow tie. Accessories include cuff links (the shirt always has French cuffs), pearl studs, dressy pumps or black patent leather shoes, and thin, black dress socks. A black silk top hat and white gloves are handsome additions.

Black-tie attire, worn at formal and semiformal weddings, consists of a black dinner jacket with matching satin-striped trousers, a gray, single- or double-breasted waistcoat or a cummerbund, and a white pleated, wing-collared shirt or a plain white, turn-down collar dress shirt—and a black bow tie. The outfit is accessorized with gold, pearl, or white studs and cuff links, thin, black dress socks and plain-toed black shoes. A black silk top hat and gray suede gloves are optional. In summer and in hot climates, a white dinner jacket may be substituted for the black one.

Daytime formal attire consists of a morning suit—a gray or black cutaway, striped trousers, a wing- or turn-down collar shirt, and a gray, single- or double-breasted waistcoat. A black-and-white striped

tie is worn with a wing-collar shirt, and a black-and-white striped four-in-hand tie with a plain white shirt. Accessories include gold, pearl, or white studs and cuff links; thin, black dress socks; and black, plain-toed shoes. A black silk top hat and gray suede gloves are optional.

For a semiformal daytime wedding, a fitted gray or black jacket is substituted for the cutaway. Everything else is the same.

At an informal wedding held during the day or at night, the men wear solid-colored business suits in gray, navy, or black, white shirts with a conservative (striped, usually) tie, and thin, black socks and black dress shoes. In summer, the groom and his attendants may wear white suits, white flannel trousers and navy jackets, or white jackets with gray trousers.

From time to time, colors become fashionable in mens' formalwear, and grooms and their attendants have been known to show up at the wedding wearing formal outfits in green, blue, cranberry, and even baby blue and pink. I still favor the more traditional outfits I have just described if only because they are insurance that your groom will look just as elegant in wedding photographs thirty years later as he does on his wedding day.

If the men's outfits are rented, the orders should be placed six to eight weeks in advance of the wedding day. If possible, a week or so before the wedding, the groom and his wedding party should go in to the store for personal fittings.

It is especially important that all the men understand the fine points of fitting suits so that all members of the wedding party will truly look not only identical but also elegant. Here are some hints:

The shirt collar should hug the neck. The shirt sleeves should extend no more than one-half inch beyond the jacket sleeve.

Jackets should button easily and not pull in any way.

Trousers should touch the vamps of shoes.

If the men are wearing light trousers, ask your groom to remind them not to wear colored underwear and to wear briefs rather than boxer shorts.

14

Be a Beautiful Bride

IF you're like most brides, you're planning to look as lovely as you possibly can when you float down the aisle. Women have been known to delay their weddings for up to a year so they can let their hair grow to the "right" length. Women who barely noticed their nails before getting engaged suddenly become obsessed with having beautiful hands for their wedding day.

Unfortunately, while you will want to look your best, you'll find it harder and harder to do as your wedding day approaches. It's all too easy to awaken on your wedding day feeling harried and looking worn out. But you don't have to—and you shouldn't. The best way not to is to incorporate a beauty routine into the weeks and days before the wedding, and stick to it. Save a few minutes each day for yourself, right from the beginning. As your wedding day nears, excuse yourself early from parties to go home and get the rest you need. It's okay, you're the guest of honor.

MAKING MAJOR IMAGE CHANGES

Think twice before making any major changes in your image before your wedding day. Getting married is change enough for most people, and besides, your groom may want to walk down the aisle with the woman he first fell in love with.

If you are determined to revamp your looks, do it as far in advance as possible. And let experts do it. This is no time to let your best friend give you a permanent or to experiment with home color.

If you're planning a haircut or a permanent, schedule it as least a month before the wedding. You'll still probably have to go back for a pre-wedding cut and set, but you'll be adjusted to your new look.

Think about simplifying your look. You'll be busy in your new life; you won't want to spend much time on maintenance—and you won't have much time for it. Consider a hairstyle that takes care of itself or requires very little from you.

Also, whatever your physical type, think about going classic, if only for a while. If you've been wearing your hair in a funky style, consider something less dramatic for your wedding day. You're going to be in a lot of pictures, which you will treasure and look at often. You'll love them more if they don't look dated six months after your wedding.

Concentrate on being healthy. Eat well, and you'll be rewarded with greater energy and luminous skin. Vow to condition your hair regularly for several months before the big day so that it is shiny and healthy-looking. Don't count on a last-minute manicure to get your hands in shape. Instead, be sure you have lots of calcium in your diet (provided by milk and milk products, and certain dark green, leafy vegetables) so that your nails are strong and long. Use the months before your wedding to establish an exercise regimen that you will follow after your marriage. No matter how busy you are now, you will be busier after you get married, so if you don't start certain regimens now, you may never find the time to do so.

Finally, do allow time for some luxurious indulgences.

☐ See a makeup specialist for advice. But do this several weeks before the wedding, so you can get used to any new cosmetics he or she recommends.
☐ Schedule a massage and facial two weeks to ten days before the wedding. Don't do this any closer to your wedding; some women's skin breaks out for a day or two afterward.
☐ Ask your hairdresser if he or she can come to your house and style your hair on your wedding day. Most will provide

this service. In fact, make appointments for everyone in your wedding party.

☐ Get a manicure every week for several weeks before your wedding—and on your wedding day, of course.

LOOKING GREAT FOR YOUR WEDDING PORTRAIT

You may want to take some extra steps to ensure that you photograph well for your formal wedding portrait. Many brides have a color and a black-and-white portrait made for their wedding. An 8½-×-10-inch glossy print is necessary if you are submitting your picture to any newspapers.

Wear a little more makeup than you might otherwise because the bright lights will wash out your skin tones, but strive for a natural look. Here are some specific tips for making up for the photographer:

☐ Use foundation or a concealer to hide skin flaws or dark circles under your eyes. Use the same shade or one only slightly lighter than your regular shade.

☐ Powder over your foundation generously to eliminate shiny spots. (Take powder to the photography session for touch-ups.) Shiny spots will photograph white.

☐ If your dress is cut low, use concealer or foundation lightly to cover flaws, and powder your shoulders and neck.

☐ Use matte eye shadow in a pastel shade. Deeper shades tend to make your eyes sink into your face, and frosted shadows will give a white cast.

☐ Use a little eyeliner to give your eyes some extra definition.

☐ Apply several coats of mascara and brush between coats to separate your lashes and keep them natural looking.

☐ If you have very light eyebrows, use short feathery strokes of an eyebrow brush to fill them in. Otherwise, brush with a little petroleum jelly to shape.

☐ Apply blush in a soft shade. You might want to use a little more for the black-and-white portrait; it adds definition to your face shape.

☐ Use a matte lipstick in a flattering shade. Pearlized shades will look too white.

☐ Even if you don't usually use hair spray, use some if necessary to make sure your hair stays in place.

MAKING UP ON YOUR WEDDING DAY

I always think the loveliest brides are the ones who look most natural. Even if you're the dramatic type and normally wear lots of eye shadow and dark lipstick, think about toning it all down for your wedding day. And if you're the type who doesn't normally wear much makeup or nail polish, stick with that. I never suggest anything more than a light pink or coral shade of nail polish for a bride, and I think clear polish is lovely, especially on short nails.

If you're the no-makeup type, though, do think about wearing a little on your wedding day, if only to heighten your color and add polish to your looks. I recommend foundation (including a concealer if you need one), well-blended eye shadow, mascara, a dusting of blush, and a light, clear-toned lipstick. Apply translucent powder so your face doesn't get shiny from excitement or from the photographer's lights. This and a very light spray of a gentle cologne—perhaps a single-flower scent—should be enough. Don't forget you'll be carrying a bouquet.

Finally, tuck your makeup in a small purse or pouch and take it with you so you can touch up during the day.

For the Groom Only

BECAUSE the groom usually has fewer prewedding responsibilities than the bride, he can be the person who sometimes spirits her away from the hectic activity that inevitably surrounds her as wedding plans proceed.

This is a time to be especially attentive to the woman you have chosen. In the weeks preceding the wedding, plan a few quiet romantic dinners alone so you can maintain the rapport that led you to this stage of your lives. Too often, couples get so caught up in the wedding preparations and festivities that they barely have time alone before the big day. If a party is planned in your honor for 8:00 P.M., take a few minutes to have a quiet drink with each other beforehand. If an early evening cocktail party is planned for you, sneak away to a quiet dinner alone afterward. Remember, you are the guests of honor at the festivities, so it is entirely proper for you to leave first.

Few grooms would forget to tell their brides how beautiful they look on their wedding day were it not for the nervousness that often besets them. Make a point of complimenting your new wife frequently during the day—after all, she has taken care to look her loveliest for you. When the inevitable compliments come to her from guests, be the first to agree. A wedding day is no time for modesty over your selection of a wife.

You do have a few things to organize before your wedding day.

You can take the initiative in planning your wedding trip. Make any transportation arrangements and set up hotel reservations well in advance.

Choose your attendants and plan and order their outfits, based on the degree of formality of the wedding. Also order your outfit for the wedding.

Arrange for your attendants' accommodations, if they live out of town. If they will be staying in a hotel, arrange to pay their bills.

The parents of the groom usually give the rehearsal dinner, so talk with your parents about the party. More information on this is in chapter 20.

With your fiancée, meet with the clergyperson who will marry you, meet with the musicians, and, of course, take your fiancée to select and then pick up the wedding rings. Needless to say, all these obligations provide the perfect opportunity for romantic lunches or dinners together.

Put your financial affairs in order. Be sure your wife will be covered by your insurance if necessary. Open any new checking or savings accounts you will need as a couple.

Buy gifts for your best man and ushers. If you are giving your bride a wedding gift other than her rings, arrange for the gift. Sometimes a woman is given heirloom jewelry from the man's family, so you may want to discuss this with your mother.

Make a date with your fiancée to pick up the marriage license. Make sure all other necessary documents—passport, birth certificate, records of blood tests—are in order.

Make plans for your bachelor party if you are giving one.

Plan to pay the clergyperson or give the money to your best man. The clergyperson should be paid the last time you meet, at the rehearsal, or just before the ceremony. Traditionally, he or she is paid from $10 to $200 depending upon local custom, the size of wedding, and your circumstances. Pay with new bills placed in a sealed envelope with the person's name written on it.

Make any necessary arrangements to move your belongings and your wedding gifts into your new home.

Arrange all transportation required for your wedding day.

During the week of the wedding, make last-minute checks to be sure every thing is in order:

☐ Recheck all documents, financial arrangements, travel arrangements, and moving plans.

☐ Be sure the men's outfits are ready and will be delivered to your home the day of the wedding.

☐ Meet with your ushers and best man to remind them of the time and date and any duties they have.

☐ Pack for your wedding trip.

☐ Show up at the church an hour before the ceremony—certainly before your bride. You may want to have the best man call her home to say you are at the church and to determine the time of her arrival, particularly if you are superstitious about seeing her before the wedding.

☐ Be sure your wedding certificate is properly signed and stored before you leave for your wedding trip.

16

Your Honeymoon

THE wedding trip you and your new husband take after the wedding is one of the best parts of getting married. The tension of the final few days evaporates, the big ceremony is over, and you are alone at last on a relaxing vacation.

Plan a trip that you will both enjoy. It is perfectly OK to follow up on an interest you share, but it won't be much fun to go skiing if one of you does not ski. Sit down together to discuss the kind of trip you have in mind. Unless one of you is an experienced traveler, you may want to forgo an adventure to new lands on your first trip together as a married couple. Are you both active, urban-oriented people? Then go to a country resort only at your own risk, or if you are both sure that round-the-clock relaxation is what you have in mind. Last of all, decide what you can reasonably afford to spend on a honeymoon.

During the planning stages, visit the offices of a travel agency to pick up some brochures on areas you think you might like to visit. Then when you start planning the trip, return to the same travel agent. This is one trip that even experienced travelers will want to go smoothly, so the services of a good agent will probably be a great help.

If you have decided to go to one place and stay for the entire time, check to see if there is a honeymoon-package price. Many hotels have special packages even for one or two nights for honeymooners, so it is to your advantage to mention that this is your wedding trip.

Most travel agents will prepare a written itinerary of your trip without your asking. Regardless of how you get it, you should have one, along with any confirmation slips and airline tickets. With everything in writing, there should be no last-minute confusion about time schedules, costs, dates, meal plans, and any extras you receive.

Finally, don't try to take off on your wedding trip or even go anywhere very far away on the day of your wedding. You will probably be too exhausted and disoriented, and this may get your entire wedding trip off to a bad start. Instead, plan to stay somewhere nearby in a nice hotel and get a leisurely start to your final destination the next day. Just be discreet about your plans so you won't be harassed by well-meaning but thoughtless friends who decide to join you on your wedding night.

LUGGAGE

If you're buying new luggage, investigate the numerous kinds before you make a final purchase. The kind of luggage you buy should be suited to your personal taste and your travel needs. If you will be taking vacations in resorts or one hotel, and will fly to your destinations, you will probably find one large Pullman suitcase that can hold up to two weeks' worth of clothes most useful. Another good piece of luggage is a small overnight bag to put under the plane seat.

If you plan to travel by train, particularly in foreign countries, you might do better with two small suitcases, since you will have to carry your own luggage most of the time.

When deciding how much luggage to take, remember the restrictions posed by your ability to carry it and the kind of transportation you usually use. You can take as much as you want if you travel by car or train. Airplanes, however, do have restrictions. Check with the travel agent or the airline to learn what their restrictions are regarding the weight that you can check without extra cost.

PACKING

Packing everything you will need and want over a one- or two-week period is no easy matter. Make a detailed list of everything you will need during your honeymoon. List clothes, personal care and health items, and recreation items (tennis racket, some good books, a game or two, a deck of cards) separately. Then set aside an entire afternoon in which to pack at a leisurely pace for your trip.

Open your empty suitcase in front of you on a bed or somewhere else. First pack the heavy items—shoes, electric rollers, hair dryer, books, purses. Wrap shoes in covers or plastic bags, and arrange them heel to toe, preferably against the hinge side of the bag.

Next roll and pack crushable separates—T-shirts, jeans, underwear, and nightgowns. Rolled clothes will not wrinkle if they are packed tightly, and they will move with the give and take of a canvas bag or duffle. Tuck rolled clothes into empty spaces and corners; use them as padding. Next pack crushables that require careful prefolding—evening clothes, dresses, skirts. Lay tissue paper or plastic bags between the items to keep them unwrinkled.

Another clever scheme for packing that takes only a little extra time involves the use of brown wrapping paper or plastic dividers that you can easily make. Buy a sheet of paper and cut pieces slightly longer than the length of your suitcase. The long ends will form handles that you can use to lift the layers of clothes and other items in and out of the suitcase. Use a pen to mark on each piece of paper what you have packed in it. Use general terms, such as *underwear, dresses,* and *first night* for the things you will want to get to as soon as you arrive somewhere.

If you are traveling somewhere by train or plane and will be separated from your large luggage, always carry a separate overnight case to ensure that you will at least have the basic things you need when you arrive. Luggage does arrive late even for honeymooners. Pack a nightgown, your beauty and health needs including your contraceptives, makeup, expensive jewelry, and your camera in the case that you plan to hand-carry. It will make life more bearable if your luggage is temporarily lost.

SPECIAL SERVICES AND TIPPING

If you want any special services—flowers, champagne, or any special food—you have only to order them when you make your final travel reservations. Remember that most honeymoon packages include either flowers or champagne, and many include both. Check this before ordering anything separately.

Almost all hotels of any size offer many special services, such as room service for food, dry cleaning and laundry, a house doctor, a concierge or ticket agent who can arrange for theater tickets or tours, bellhops who take your luggage to and from your room, and a doorman who greets you and removes your luggage, generally putting it into the hands of the bellhop. Since it is your honeymoon, just relax and take advantage of these services, remembering that tips are required somewhere along the way to compensate the people who wait on you.

The doorman is tipped at arrival or departure for loading your car and each time he hails a cab for you or gets your car.

The desk clerk is the next person you come into contact with. He does not receive a tip, but if you are going to pay with a credit card, you should tell him when you arrive.

The bellhop who carries the bag to your room should be tipped per bag, depending upon how much he does for you.

The concierge or ticket broker need not be tipped anything, since he takes his commission from the tickets or tour he sells you.

A waiter who brings anything from room service—which can vary from predinner drinks to a complete meal or a late-night snack—is tipped 10–15 percent of the bill. Tell him when you want him to return to pick up the tray, or, if you do not want to be disturbed, place the tray outside your door.

The person who cleans your room each day should be left a tip for each day.

In the hotel dining room, you tip as you would at any restaurant or night club. If the maître d'hôtel arranges a better table for you or gives you any extra assistance, a tip of at least $5 is required. If he only checks your reservations and shows you to your table, no tip is expected. Waiters receive 15 percent of the total food and drink bill. The headwaiter—the man who takes your order and explains the French on the menu—receives an additional 5 percent tip.

If during your stay you have cause to complain about noise or something in the room, call the assistant manager, who runs the front desk. Only if he does not offer assistance should you call the manager.

If you need something special—mending supplies, extra blankets, or ice, for example—call the housekeeper. She is also the person to call if you leave something in the room and notice it when you are 100 miles away.

Allow enough time to check out. Generally half an hour is enough. If you will be leaving after checkout time, you may be able to extend your checkout time, or you can check your luggage with the bell captain until you are ready to leave.

Above all, relax and enjoy your honeymoon. It's a break from the hectic pace of your prewedding days and a time to be together without any responsibilities before you settle into your new daily life. When you're back home, you can discuss the possibility of putting the tooth-paste cap back on the tube or the necessity of using a clothes hamper, but not now, not during this romantic hiatus in your life.

You will also want to take care not to smother in togetherness. Often honeymooners think something is wrong if they want to leave their room before noon or, heaven forbid, if one of them wants to go off alone for a few hours. Leave lots of time for long, romantic dinners *à deux,* but don't be hurt or surprised if you or your new mate wants to go buy a newspaper or even go shopping alone.

17

Your Wedding Gifts

WEDDING gifts are expressions of people's pleasure and joy in your marriage. They should be accepted in the same spirit in which they are given—even if you do get three identical casseroles and an atrocious dish that your great-aunt Minnie has been saving for you for twenty years.

If your wedding is large, you will receive many gifts, which means that you will have to devote a fair amount of your prewedding hours to writing thank-you notes. Your wedding gifts should give you much pleasure for many years to come, and they will, too, if you organize yourself properly to receive them and follow a few simple procedures for ensuring that you mostly receive gifts that match your taste, wants, and needs.

As soon as possible after your wedding plans have been announced, register your gift preferences. Try to register at a major department store, preferably where you live and in a town where most of your guests and family live. If you wish, you may also register your gift preferences at camping, sporting, antique, plant, or aquarium shops, or any other shop that carries your gift preferences. Many brides register at a department store for formal china; sterling or some other kind of formal flatware; crystal glassware; everyday dishes, flatware and glassware; bed and table linens; appliances; and cookware. For more specialized items, you may register at a small store or boutique that carries goods you like. Most of your selections will be a matter of practicality and need, but especially when choosing tableware, it is helpful to know something about the choices available to you.

CHINA

The word *china* is popularly used for all kinds of dinnerware, although officially it refers only to fine china, which is either porcelain or bone. Fine china is expensive, extremely hard, nonporous, and translucent. Initially white, it is painted in a wide assortment of lovely patterns. Too often a bride receives fine china and then fails to use it regularly. When you have something so lovely, why deny yourself the pleasure of seeing it on your table? Most chinas are durable enough to be washed in a dishwasher with a reliable detergent.

Other dishes you may want to receive as gifts include:

Earthenware and stoneware, which are available in a large variety of patterns. These dishes are suitable for everything from today's "formal" dinner to the most casual kind of dining. Both kinds of dishes are thicker than china, not translucent, and less expensive. Earthenware is also soft and chips easily. Stoneware is harder and denser and is frequently found only in service dishes and tea or coffee pots.

Melamine is a practical plastic dishware that does not chip or break. It is light, comes in a wide variety of patterns, and has a lustrous look to it.

Dishes are sold in three ways: open stock, by the piece, and in place settings. Open stock means that the dishes are expected to be available from the manufacturer over a continuing period of time. If this is important to you, ask whether the pattern you select is open stock. Manufacturers will not guarantee open stock, however, and occasionally brides do buy something only to find that it is difficult to replace in a few years. Selecting an old, established china pattern offers some protection against this. If it is taken off open stock, you can sometimes find replacement dishes at auctions or through companies that specialize in selling old china patterns.

Dishes can be purchased in place settings or individually. A place setting typically consists of a dinner plate, salad or dessert plate, cup and saucer, and soup bowl or butter plate, according to your preference. There is no savings in price if dishes are bought in place settings. Brides usually receive dishes in place settings, but you might pass the word that you need individual pieces, that is, dessert plates or luncheon plates.

CHOOSING GLASSWARE

Most brides need and receive glassware. It may take the form of casual, everyday glasses, and you may also want to register for crystal glassware. There are various kinds of crystal—some of which does not ring when tapped even though it is very fine—and glassware.

Whether you choose a fine crystal pattern or another kind of glassware, you will probably need water glasses, wineglasses, juice glasses, and bar glasses according to your entertaining needs. Especially thoughtful is a present of fine liqueur glasses or brandy snifters.

Crystal may be selected from among the more elaborate cutglass patterns, or a simpler pattern may be chosen, depending upon how formally you will be entertaining and your taste. Before you select elaborate cut-glass or colored wineglasses, remember that wine is usually drunk in plain glasses so the imbibers may observe and appreciate its color.

CHOOSING FLATWARE

Sterling silverware has become so expensive in recent years that many brides have turned to the equally beautiful and lasting silverplate and pewter. There are also many lovely stainless steel patterns; in fact, stainless steel has become the most popular choice of brides today. Flatware comes in a variety of patterns and should be chosen to coordinate with your dishes and glassware. It is sold in place settings or by the individual piece. A place setting consists of a dinner fork, salad fork (which doubles as a fish and dessert fork), teaspoon, soup or place spoon, and dinner knife. A soupspoon usually has a rounded bowl and is used only for soup, whereas a place spoon, which does not, can also be used as a soup, dessert, and place spoon. Apart from enough place settings for your needs (most brides want eight to twelve), you may also want extra salad forks and teaspoons, as well as matching service pieces.

REGISTERING AT THE BRIDAL REGISTRY

A week or so before you register your gift preferences, visit the department store of your choice and pick up brochures on dishes, glasses, and silver. When you are making your final decisions, you may want to visit the store again and ask to see your choices in a table setting, to be sure everything coordinates.

When you are ready to list your gift preferences, make an appointment to talk with a bridal consultant. Bridal registry is a free service provided by most department stores and many small specialty housewares stores.

Persons invited to your wedding call the store or visit it to choose your gift. In stores where you are registered, careful records of what has been purchased for you are kept so that duplication of gifts can be avoided as much as possible.

When a registry is used, there are also no problems in returning or exchanging gifts. A smart bride registers at the main department store in her town, at another one in the town where most of her parents' or the groom's parents' friends live, and possibly at one or two small, specialized stores whose name she can pass along to close friends who make inquiries about her needs. Try to select gifts in all price ranges.

As gifts begin to arrive, check in every week or so with the registry to be sure that those you have received are removed from the list.

The consultant at a bridal registry is usually highly knowledgeable in housewares and fine dinner table appointments. If you don't know much about buying these things, this is the person to ask.

DISPLAYING GIFTS

Brides sometimes arrange displays of gifts in their homes so they can be viewed by friends and wedding guests. To do this you will need tables on which to display the gifts. In some large cities, a bridal consultant at the department store can tell you where tables can be rented, or you can build your own, using plywood and wood sawhorses. The tables are covered with white or pastel floor-length cloths, so it doesn't matter what they look like under the covers. White rayon satin is reasonably priced and makes an excellent covering for the tables; you need not even hem it—just buy it longer than the tables and tuck the ends under for a soft effect.

Arranging wedding gifts calls for no small degree of tact. Two lovely but inexpensive potholders shouldn't be placed next to a place setting of sterling. If you received five crockpots, display only one so the duplication is not obvious. As a rule, a place setting of china, silverware, and glassware is set up once on the display tables.

Remove the givers' cards from presents. Presents of money are noted on a white card, on which the giver's name and the word *check* are written, never the amount.

Some brides do not wish to display their wedding gifts. This is entirely a personal choice, and you as the bride should make your own decision regarding this. But remember that many of your friends and relatives will truly be interested in seeing your presents. If you're moving out of town after your marriage, this may be their only chance to share in your future household.

As you open your presents for display, keep the boxes they come in, so you can use them later when you pack the gifts to move them to your new home.

INSURING PRESENTS

If you receive many presents, you will need insurance on them. An insurance company will furnish you with a floating policy, which usually lasts three months and covers any damages incurred during

shipping. A further precaution, if your wedding has been widely pub-
licized or announced in any newspaper, is to hire a guard for those
times when you will be away from the house overnight or when you
are attending a party in your honor that has been announced in newspapers. The guard should, of course, sit with the gifts during the
rehearsal dinner, wedding, and reception. Contact your local police
department or a private agency to find a reliable guard.

EXCHANGING PRESENTS

If you receive very many presents, there will undoubtedly be some
duplications. You can never ask someone who gave you a gift to return
it—indeed, the giver should never know that his or her gift was the
same as someone else's.

Keep the small notices usually posted inside wedding-gift boxes
from big department stores to make it easy to return unwanted items.
Most practical and convenient is to wait until after the wedding to
return the gifts. Then you can sort out everything you have received
and better organize those presents you must exchange.

Highly personalized gifts that you don't happen to like generally
should not be returned, even if they aren't to your taste. If your Aunt
Sarah gives you a hideous one-of-a-kind soup tureen, she will expect
to see it when she visits you. And to be tactful, you should display
it, if only for her visit. But it would be silly to keep a collection of five
identical saucepans. Return the four you won't need.

If a gift arrives damaged from a store and is insured, write the giver
so that he or she can make the necessary adjustments for replacement.
If a gift arrives damaged and was obviously hand-wrapped by the
sender and not insured, simply write a gracious thank-you note as if
the gift had arrived in perfect condition.

THANK-YOU NOTES

For every gift you receive, you must send a personal handwritten
thank-you note. If your wedding is going to be very large, and if it is
impossible for you to keep up with the thank-you notes as you go

along, a printed notice indicating that you have received the gift can be sent, but these never replace a handwritten note. Such notes can usually be purchased in the stationery department of any large department store. They read as follows:

---

greatly appreciates your gift and will take pleasure in writing a personal thank-you note later.

Thank-you notes are usually written on informals—small sheets of notepaper folded in half. They are printed with your name or monogram, or can be plain white or another attractive color. Notes written after the wedding can be imprinted with your new name.

If you are not changing your name, then any notes you have printed prior to your wedding with your maiden name on them will be fine afterward, or you might want to follow the newer custom of having informals printed with a joint monogram—that is, using both your initials. Usually such monograms consist of two initials, for each of your surnames, separated by a dot or some other typographical device.

A thank-you note should be personal. Mention the gift and, if possible, how you intend to use it in your new home. Sample notes follow:

Dear Aunt Jane,

You and Uncle Joe were so kind to send Jim and me the lovely silver serving dish. Both of us admire it and look forward to using it at many dinners. We look forward to seeing you at the wedding.

Affectionately,
Jackie

Dear Mrs. Wells,

Our thanks to you for the beautiful vase. It has been given a place of honor on a table in our new living room.

We appreciate your kindness in remembering us with such a truly beautiful gift.

We enjoyed seeing you at the wedding.

Fondly,
Jackie

After you are married, your husband can help you by writing some of the thank-you notes. Whoever is writing mentions both of you but signs only his or her name. Notes can be dated in the upper-right-hand corner or at the end of the note on the left side of the page.

Thank-you notes must be written within three months after the wedding day. People have put a great deal of effort and thought into getting you a present you will appreciate. It is up to you to make them feel appreciated in your gracious thank-you note.

18
The Wedding Festivities

EVERYONE likes weddings in part because they present such a great opportunity for parties. Most weddings are the occasion of several festivities other than the main event—a shower or two and a rehearsal dinner, at minimum. If you are socially active, then there may be even more celebrating—more showers, a bride's luncheon, a bachelor party, and dinner parties in your honor. The trend today is to entertain both sexes at evening parties rather than at traditional showers.

You can never ask anyone to give you a party; your friends and relatives must offer. With a few exceptions, noted below, you can accept the offer of anyone who wants to have a party for you.

Usually, the parties are designed to satisfy different sets of friends— your cousins, your work friends, your college roommates, your child-hood friends. It's up to you to see that the same people are not invited over and over again to parties in your honor, especially if gifts are expected. When someone such as your sister or a bridesmaid will be invited to all the parties, you should let her know after the first one that no further presents are expected. After giving one shower present, the person can attend without giving a gift, or can give a small, token present.

THE ENGAGEMENT PARTY

The engagement party, which is described in greater detail in chapter 2, is one of the few parties given by your parents, although it may be given by the groom's parents or other close relatives or friends—or all of the above.

THE BRIDE'S LUNCHEON

This special event, which, I'm sorry to say, is held less and less often these days, is typically scheduled a few days before the wedding, when all the wedding party has arrived. Designed to honor the bride's attendants, the party includes the mothers and sisters of the bride and groom, close relatives such as aunts and cousins, and any close friends who would be especially honored to attend. It may be given by the bride, but is often given by her mother, an aunt, or a close friend of her mother. The bridesmaids may also give the party.

Guests do not bring presents. Instead, the bride gives her wedding party the presents she has bought to thank them.

The traditional cake for this party is frosted pink and has a ring or a thimble baked into it. Its recipient is said to be the next bride. This is also a time to show off your trousseau or wedding gifts, if you choose.

These days, the bride and groom sometimes prefer to give their attendants a party jointly. Such a party is usually held in the evening, but it can be a luncheon. It provides a perfect opportunity for the members of the wedding party to get to know each other. When a joint party is given, the couple can incorporate as many or as few traditions as they choose.

THE BACHELOR PARTY

If the groom chooses, he can have a bachelor party, or his friends may plan one for him. It is usually held the night before the rehearsal dinner or even the night before the wedding, although this custom is waning, and the dinner is now given a week or so before the wedding to ensure good health and alertness on the part of all attending the wedding. The groom's party is traditionally a boisterous one, with many toasts, excessive drinking, and other shenanigans, and the custom of holding it several days rather than the night before the wedding is one that pleases me.

The bride is toasted, usually with glasses that are tossed over the men's shoulders after they are emptied. If this custom is followed, arrangements for it should be made with the restaurant or club where the party is held.

This is also an occasion for the groom to present his groomsmen with presents and to announce any last-minute arrangements to his groomsmen.

GIFTS FOR ATTENDANTS

As soon as possible before the wedding, plan the gifts you want to give your attendants. The best man and maid of honor are usually given slightly different and sometimes more expensive gifts than are the other attendants. The gifts you choose should be a significant reminder of your wedding; frequently they are engraved. Allow a minimum of four weeks for engraving. Wrap the gifts in pretty paper and ribbons before presenting them.

The maid of honor or best man might receive a gold or silver signature ring or a sterling key ring. Charms, small pins, lockets, and bracelets are excellent gifts for bridesmaids. Ushers will appreciate small leather items, cuff links, money clips, pen-and-pencil sets, or tie tacks.

Especially thoughtful is the custom of giving the mothers and fathers small remembrances of the occasion. They can be small personal items similar to the attendants' gifts.

BRIDAL SHOWERS

Showers are parties given in honor of the bride. They are usually afternoon or early evening events; refreshments are served, and decorations, if used, should be light and gay. You may serve tea foods or other light refreshments or a meal, depending upon the time of the party.

Only close friends and relatives of the bride and groom and their families are invited.

The old rule that a relative should never give a shower seems to have faded into oblivion. Most women have a loving aunt or cousin who wants to entertain for them, and there is no reason not to do so. Immediate members of the family—sisters and mothers—still do not give showers, although they can have another party where gifts are not expected.

Shower Gifts

Shower gifts need not rival wedding gifts. A considerate bride and hostess will frequently pass the word among potential guests that gifts are to be small.

Frequently showers are planned around a gift category: linen, china, kitchenware, bathroom accessories, or personal gifts, such as lingerie, may be specified by the hostess. If a shower is given jointly for the bride and groom, the presents are always for the household; gifts of a personal nature are not given at such showers. Gifts may be centered around a couple's special interests, such as wine, sailing, cooking out, or fine food.

Thank-Yous

Each person is, of course, thanked when a gift is opened and again when he or she leaves the party. It is nice to write a thank-you note but not necessary unless someone sent a gift and did not attend the shower. Most important, send a personal note or even a gift to the person who gave the shower in your honor. Thank-you notes should always be handwritten.

OTHER PARTIES

Sometimes parties—not showers—are given to honor the bride and groom. Gifts are not expected; the only obligation is to enjoy oneself. Such parties are frequently planned to entertain out-of-town guests who arrive before the wedding day. They can be breakfasts, lunches, cocktail parties, or dinner parties.

Page 218 of the Bride's Organizer will help you keep track of all the prewedding festivities.

19
Ceremonies Within
Ceremonies

MARRIAGE ceremonies vary from religion to religion, but most consist of two parts: the exchange of vows and the exchange of rings. Your clergyperson will be familiar with your religion's service, but you may want to read the service, too, before you meet with him or her to make any final decisions. If so, at your first meeting, ask for a copy of the service and inquire about any changes, additions, or deletions that are possible.

PROTESTANT CEREMONY

In some Protestant churches, the congregation stands when the bride comes down the aisle and remains standing for all or part of the service.

Two new touches have slipped into Protestant ceremonies over the last few years: the custom of the father kissing the bride at the altar as he gives her away, which is entirely a matter of personal choice, and the ceremony in which the couple kneels to say the Lord's Prayer at the altar near the end of the ceremony. Discuss this with your clergyperson, as special arrangements will have to be made if you want this included in the ceremony.

EPISCOPAL CEREMONY

At least one partner must be a baptized Christian to marry in the Episcopal Church. By Church law, you must give at least thirty days notice of your intention to marry. It is customary, however, to inform the Rector as soon as you know so that there will be ample time to plan. The Rector will also want to conduct some premarital counseling. Weddings are not encouraged during Lent or on Sundays.

During the processional, the bride takes her father's left arm. As they reach the chancel steps, the father gives his daughter to the priest, who in turn bestows her on the groom at the appropriate moment in the ceremony. Then the bride and groom, accompanied by their main attendants (witnesses), go to the altar together to exchange vows.

If both the bride and groom wish, the Holy Eucharist may be included in the service. Guests remain standing throughout the ceremony, except when kneeling to take communion. (Those who are not taking communion simply take their seats while the others are kneeling.)

JEWISH CEREMONY

The Jewish faith has three groups—Orthodox, Conservative, and Reformed. The ceremony varies depending upon the affiliation of the couple.

A Jewish wedding is often held at the place of the reception—a hotel, private club, or home—although there has been a move back toward holding weddings in synagogues. It is usually not held on Saturday, the Jewish Sabbath.

Among the Orthodox and Conservative Jews, a couple is married standing under a *chuppah,* or wedding canopy. Usually both parents accompany the bride and groom in the processional, and the parents walk together in the recessional. They stand slightly behind or beside their children during the ceremony, facing their guests. The bride stands to the right of the groom. Among the Orthodox and Conservative groups, part of the ceremony is in Hebrew; most Reform weddings are primarily in English. Wine is sipped by the bride and groom during the ceremony. At the end of it, the groom (and these days sometimes

Processional for a Jewish wedding

the liberated bride) crushes a wineglass wrapped in a napkin—although in reality, a light bulb is substituted for a wineglass to reduce the risk of cutting the groom.

Reform Jews sometimes dispense with the wedding canopy and the crushing of the wineglass, although there is a trend toward more, rather than less, tradition in all religious ceremonies.

All men attending the Jewish wedding ceremony wear skullcaps or street hats. Skullcaps are furnished at the synagogue for guests who don't have them.

ROMAN CATHOLIC CEREMONY

The father of the bride does not give the bride away. He escorts her to the chancel steps, her maid of honor lifts her veil so her father can kiss her, and she joins the groom at the altar. Some couples are choosing to be greeted by the priest at the vestibule door so he can lead the processional.

Traditional wedding marches, which are secular music, are not allowed in many Catholic churches.

A nuptial mass, into which the wedding ceremony is incorporated, can be arranged for almost any Catholic wedding. Non-Catholics do not take communion, nor does the non-Catholic member of the couple, if the marriage is mixed.

If there is room, all the attendants step past the altar rail during the ceremony; otherwise only the maid of honor and the best man accompany the bride and groom past the steps. It is customary for the main attendants to be Catholic.

A final touching ceremony within the Catholic wedding may occur when the bride walks back to the left of the main altar to offer her bouquet to the Virgin Mary. She then rejoins her husband for the recessional.

QUAKER CEREMONY

A Quaker wedding is performed during a regular meeting of the congregation. Today's Quaker bride wears a traditional white wedding gown and veil, although it is usually fairly simple, in keeping with Quaker religious views. No bridal party is required, although this is becoming common today. The couple enters the meeting together and sits facing the congregation. After the traditional silence, the couple joins hands and repeats the vows to each other. The father of the bride does not give her away, and no one officiates at the wedding. The couple may conclude the ceremony with a kiss. After they sit down, the marriage certificate is brought out to be signed after it is read to the congregation. The meeting continues for another half-hour or so.

This ceremony is in keeping with the Quaker view that marriage is a personal and individual commitment, made in the presence of God and friends who witness the ceremony. A Quaker betrothal is announced publicly at meetings several times, usually over a period of three months before the ceremony.

Marriage certificates are treasured documents in Quaker families. Some have been handed down through five and six generations.

A Quaker reception, usually held at the church or in the bride's home, is traditionally kept simple.

EASTERN ORTHODOX CEREMONY

Many Russians, Eastern Europeans, and some Mediterranean people are members of the Eastern Orthodox church, which is ceremonially similar to the Roman Catholic church but does not recognize the pope as the titular head of the church.

Some Eastern Orthodox denominations require that the banns be published three times before the day of the wedding. Sometimes a betrothal service at which rings are exchanged is held.

The processional and recessional are like those of any other wedding. The father of the bride gives her away and then returns to the pew where his wife is seated.

MORMON CEREMONY

Two kinds of weddings are held by Mormons: a religious ceremony in a temple of the church, which is available only to those who meet certain requirements, and a civil ceremony, which may be performed by a clergyperson of the church or a civil official. Frequently persons who are married in a civil ceremony are remarried later in the church, after they have met all the requirements.

The vows at a Mormon wedding are taken "for time and all eternity" rather than "until death do you part," as in Christian weddings.

CHRISTIAN SCIENCE CEREMONY

Christian Science readers are not ordained ministers, so persons of this faith are usually married in a Protestant church. If one of the couple is not a Christian Scientist, the couple is generally married in that person's church. If both are Christian Scientists, they should find a clergyperson whom they like and ask him or her to marry them. Protestant clergypersons are aware of the restriction and will usually as a courtesy marry a Christian Science couple. Since the two are not regular congregants, the clergyperson should be generously paid for his or her services.

AMISH CEREMONY

The Amish ceremony always takes place on either a Tuesday or a Thursday, and usually in the month of November.

On the day of the wedding, friends, relatives, and neighbors start arriving by 8:00 A.M. At 8:30 the ceremony begins, usually with the chanting of hymns. Then a minister preaches for forty-five minutes, after which a bishop gives the traditional wedding sermon, which lasts for over an hour. When the sermon is completed, the bride and groom are summoned by the bishop to the front of the congregation. After a ten-minute wedding ceremony, the congregation kneels for prayer and a dismissal hymn.

No special wedding attire is worn by the bride or groom; Sunday best doubles as the wedding dress.

The ceremony usually lasts until noon, at which time the backless benches are converted into tables, which are then spread with a feast of delicious food—all prepared the day before. The guests, who may number 500 or more, spend the remainder of the day in feasting and merrymaking.

THE DOUBLE WEDDING

Often sisters or friends who are especially close choose to be married in a double ceremony. The format of invitations for such a wedding is discussed in chapter 9.

Each bride has her own maid of honor, although the brides may, and frequently do, act as each other's honor attendants. Other attendants are generally shared, or there may be two sets. If there are two sets of attendants, they need not dress alike, although their outfits should be color-coordinated or thematically tied together. Similarly, the brides need not wear identical dresses, but one should not be more formally dressed than the other, and their dresses should be somewhat similar in style. All male members of the wedding parties dress alike.

The only other problems unique to a double wedding are the processional and recessional and who does what first. Generally the latter problem is solved by rank—the older bride goes down the aisle first, and she and her fiancé say their vows first, although everything apart from the vows is read only once. (This is only one solution to the problem; brides could draw lots or arrange their order alphabetically.) Generally the older bride stands to the left with her attendants. The younger bride stands to the right with her attendants.

The processional goes as follows: the grooms enter with the clergyperson and the best men. Both sets of ushers, paired by height, lead the processional. The female attendants of the first bride, then the bride and her father, follow. The second bride's attendants and the bride and her escort then proceed down the aisle. If the brides are friends, each father accompanies the bride. If they are sisters, another close relative escorts the second bride down the aisle, but the father first gives away the older daughter and then moves to the younger daughter to give her away. At the recessional, the parties may leave separately as they entered, or the couples may leave followed by both sets of attendants.

At the reception, if the brides are friends, two lines may be formed in the traditional way, or a joint receiving line can be formed, which is set up in this way: mother of older bride, mother of older bride's groom, mother of younger bride, mother of younger bride's groom, older bride and her husband, her honor attendant, younger bride and her husband, her honor attendant, bridesmaids.

WEDDINGS INVOLVING CLERGYPERSONS

If a clergyperson is a member of either the bride's or the groom's family, it is appropriate but not required for that person to perform the ceremony. If a father officiates at his daughter's wedding, he does not give her away; her mother does this on behalf of both of them. The bride is escorted down the aisle by a brother, uncle, godfather, or close family friend.

If either the bride or groom is a clergyperson, the marriage ceremony can be held at the other's church or temple. Alternately, it can be held in the clergyperson's own church or temple, where either his or her immediate superior or another clergyperson of equal or superior rank officiates.

Only a rare bride who is a clergyperson may choose not to wear a wedding dress, so the question of whether to wear a clerical collar is moot, but the groom who is a clergyperson may, if he chooses, wear his clerical collar with formal dress. He may also wear regular formal dress sans a clerical collar. Vestments are not worn by any member of the wedding party. A family member who officiates at a wedding changes into whatever dress is required for the reception.

MILITARY WEDDINGS

A man who is a member of the armed forces may choose to be married in uniform. Most likely, several of his attendants will also be in uniform. A wedding party may also be mixed, with some ushers in uniform and some not. The ushers not in uniform wear whatever is appropriate to the formality and time of day of the wedding. Men in uniform never wear a boutonniere.

Few gestures are as dramatic as the arch of swords that military ushers form as a tribute to the bride and groom. If the ushers are going to form the arch of swords, it is done outside the church door immediately after the wedding if the weather is nice or, if not, at the foot of the chancel steps. If the sword ceremony takes place inside, the ushers line up and at the command "Draw swords" from the head usher in uniform, swords are drawn blade up to form an arch under which the bride and groom walk. Civilian ushers stand in line at attention during this brief ceremony. The ushers return their swords to their sheaths, and then escort the bridesmaids in the recessional. (Bridesmaids always walk on the right, since the swords are worn on the left.) If the sword ceremony is outdoors, the bridesmaids walk up the aisle alone or in pairs while the ushers quickly leave by a side door and go to the front steps of the church.

The rank of the groom—and the bride if she is in the armed forces—is listed on the invitations and announcements, as noted in chapter 9.

20
The Rehearsal

THE rehearsal is held, of course, at the church or place of your wedding. The rehearsal dinner may be held in someone's home or at a restaurant. It can be as formal or as informal as you want.

Since the members of your wedding party may not know each other, and since there seems to be something inherently tense about a rehearsal, an especially good tactic is to invite the wedding party to your house for drinks and hors d'oeuvres beforehand. Allow the group an hour or so together in this relaxed setting and your rehearsal will go more smoothly. When everyone is already in a party mood, there is less likelihood that the rehearsal will become drawn out.

Until a few years ago, superstition prevented a bride from participating directly in the rehearsal, and a bridesmaid or sister stood in for her. Few brides worry about this today. After all, no star is expected to take the stage without a dress rehearsal. The minister will usually direct the rehearsal anyway, and he will be aware, from previous meetings with you, of any special touches you and your fiancé want.

A rehearsal is just what it sounds like—a chance for the bride and groom and all the members of the wedding party to practice what they will do during the wedding ceremony. You will probably want two or three walk-throughs to be sure that each person understands what he or she is expected to do. In addition, the attendants (except the flower girl and ring bearer, who are simply told where and when to report to the church) should each be given a list of their responsibilities. If possible, type the lists neatly. These lists can also be passed out and discussed at your house before the rehearsal or at the dinner afterward. Following are sample lists:

The Best Man

1. Help the groom dress for the ceremony (which means you must be dressed well in advance yourself).
2. Get the clergyperson's fee in a plain, sealed envelope from the groom and deliver it to the clergyperson.
3. Remind the groom of the marriage license, airline tickets, and any documents he needs.
4. Sign the marriage license as the groom's witness.
5. Get the groom to the church before the ceremony, then keep him from going to pieces while waiting in the vestry.
6. Carry the ring in your waistcoat pocket, ready to hand to the groom at the proper moment.
7. Take the groom's gloves as he waits for the bride at the chancel steps. (Take your own off, too, if it reduces possible fumbling for the ring.)
8. Offer the first toast to the bride and groom (at both the rehearsal dinner and reception).
9. Make sure the going-away car is safely hidden away.
10. Help the bride and groom get away from the reception.
11. Return the groom's wedding clothes to his home or to the rental shop.

Maid or Matron of Honor

1. Act as the bride's witness for the marriage license.
2. Help the bride with her gloves, train, veil, flowers, prayer book, etc., during the ceremony.
3. Hold the groom's wedding band and give it to bride or clergyperson at the appropriate moment in the ceremony.
4. Stand in the receiving line to greet guests.

Ushers

1. Arrive at the church at the designated time.
2. Light the aisle candelabra fifteen minutes before the ceremony.
3. Seat the guests.
4. Take down the pew ribbons as you come to each new section.
5. Pull the aisle runner into position and pull it back at the end of the ceremony.
6. Walk in the processional and recessional.
7. Return to escort the bride's mother and father and the groom's mother and father out. Then return to take out the rest of the guests an aisle at a time by standing before the aisle to move out.
8. At the reception, each usher takes a turn dancing with the bride and the bridesmaids. They should make sure there are no wallflowers.

Bridesmaids

1. Help the bride in any way they can with errands.
2. Entertain for the bride, usually by giving her a shower.
3. Stand in the receiving line to greet guests.

Flower Girl and Ring Bearer

The flower girl may strew rose petals or flowers along the aisle, and the ring bearer's official job is to carry the wedding rings to the altar. Most weddings go more smoothly if these tasks are dispensed with, and the children simply march in the processional. Often very young children do not march in the recessional but join their parents in their pews at the end of the ceremony.

It is especially thoughtful to send notes to the attendants the week before the wedding listing the times and places you will need them. This is also a good time to tell them of any transportation arrangements you have made for them.

WALKING THROUGH THE CEREMONY

Before the rehearsal, you will probably want to be somewhat familiar with the steps of the wedding ceremony.

Choosing the aisle for the processional and recessional is the first order of business. Usually the center aisle is used, if there is one. If there are two aisles, choose the one that is most convenient for you, or use one for the processional and another for the recessional. Note: This may not work if you have white aisle carpet and only want to decorate one aisle.

Once the rehearsal begins, the minister will position everyone at the front of the church as they will stand during the ceremony. Then everyone will practice standing where they should be after the vows are taken, when the recessional is about to begin. As soon as everyone is sure of his or her position during the ceremony, the groom and best man may want to practice entering from the side of the church, where they will have been awaiting the start of the processional music.

While they are doing this, the other attendants can assemble at the back of the church to practice the processional. Everyone stands in the order of his or her scheduled appearance—the ushers, who can enter singly or in pairs; the bridesmaids, who also enter singly or in pairs; the matron of honor; the ring bearer and flower girl, who usually walk together; and finally the bride and her father. Attendants usually pace themselves about six to ten feet apart. The bride waits until the last attendants are about halfway down the aisle, or she may wait until they are all at the altar before starting down the aisle. The processional and recessional should be practiced with music, if possible.

You, the bride, usually walk on your father's right, taking his arm as you go down the aisle. When you reach the chancel steps, relinquish your father's arm, move your bouquet to your left hand, and wait until

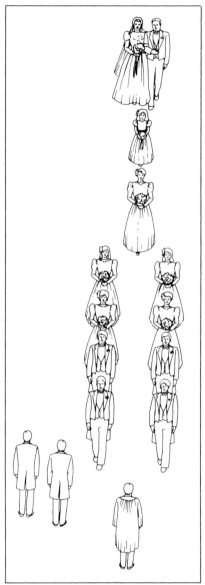

Processional for a formal or semiformal wedding

the clergyperson asks who gives you in marriage. Your father replies, "I do," or "Her mother and I do," and then takes his place beside your mother in her pew. In Catholic weddings, where the father doesn't give the bride away, he returns to his pew and sits down immediately after escorting his daughter down the aisle.

In a Jewish wedding, where the parents often participate in the processional and recessional, the rabbi will offer suggestions about where everyone should stand.

Once you have reached the front of the sanctuary, you usually hand your flowers to your honor attendant, who may, before taking them, turn back your veil. In a Jewish ceremony or a Roman Catholic ceremony where a mass will be said, the bride's veil is turned back at the start of the ceremony so she can share the wine or take Communion; in a Protestant ceremony, her veil may not be turned back until the end of the ceremony so that she may kiss her husband. Either way, her maid or matron of honor turns back her veil.

When the rings are about to be exchanged, the bride turns to her maid of honor, and the groom to his best man, to get the rings. Alternately, they may have been given to the clergyperson prior to the ceremony for safekeeping.

Generally, the part of the vows that requires a response from you and the groom will be repeated several times during the rehearsal. When the clergyperson has pronounced you husband and wife and congratulated you, you may embrace and kiss briefly. A passionate embrace is out of place. The bride is kissed at the altar because the groom traditionally is the first person to kiss his wife. If you and the groom will go immediately to the reception and bypass all guests who might kiss you, you need not kiss at the altar—although this is a custom that few people forgo. After the embrace, take back your bouquet from your maid of honor and start the recessional. If you have a train, the maid of honor may start it as you walk up the aisle. (You might also have someone posted at the back of the church to start your train in the processional.) Walk with dignity during the recessional. The music will be faster than in the processional, and you will be feeling elated, joyous, maybe even relieved, but this is no reason to sprint up the aisle. Generally the maid of honor and the best man are paired during the recessional, and the bridesmaids pair up with ushers. If you don't want people paired off, it is your decision.

After a couple of run-throughs of the ceremony, the processional, and the recessional, everyone meets at the front of the church to

Recessional for a formal or semiformal wedding

discuss any questions and so the ushers can be briefed on the proper way to seat guests.

SEATING GUESTS

At a large formal wedding, the guests are seated in a rather ceremonial manner, and ushers should be told how to go about seating guests during the rehearsal.

As guests arrive, they are greeted at the entrance to the sanctuary by the ushers. (More and more frequently these days, they are also greeted by the bride's and the groom's parents, who stay in the front hall or just outside the church or synagogue to receive their guests informally. It is a warm custom that I hope takes hold.)

Wedding guests are traditionally seated to one side or the other in a sanctuary, depending upon whether they are family or friends of the groom (right side) or of the bride (left side). It is a good idea to dispense with this custom of choosing sides if the guest list is unbalanced or if the bride and groom or their families have many friends in common.

Another custom is to provide special seating for close family and friends. Several front pews are ribboned off, and guests receive a small handwritten or printed card marked Within the Ribbons with their invitations. They present the card to the usher or, at a large wedding, the ushers may keep a list of those who are to be seated in this way. As the first persons are seated within the ribbons, the usher removes the ribbons.

A custom that is being pleasantly updated is the manner in which ushers escort guests to their seats. An usher traditionally offers his arm to the woman of a couple and escorts her down the aisle, while her husband follows behind. When a group of women appear together, the usher offers his arm to the oldest woman present. A more modern way of seating guests, however, is for the usher to walk ahead of a couple or group. This way, a woman can take her husband's arm, and the oldest woman in a group is spared the rather dubious compliment of the usher's arm. Exceptions do exist: a dowager aunt who obviously expects to be escorted by an usher, or an infirm, elderly person of either sex, or a nubile teenager are among those who are respectively, pleased, relieved, and flattered to be offered an usher's arm. No usher should be so lacking in gallantry that he cannot make individual decisions about whom to usher personally to their seats. At small, informal weddings, guests often seat themselves.

During the last few minutes before the ceremony starts, grandparents are ushered in and seated in the second or third pew. Five minutes before the start of the ceremony, the groom's parents are seated on the right in the first or second pew. Since the bride's mother will be seated shortly, if she has not already come to the back of the sanctuary, the head usher goes to the room where the best man and groom are waiting, to alert them that the ceremony is about to begin. He then returns and escorts the bride's mother to the first or second pew on the left. If he is ushering, her own son seats her. The mother of the bride is usually accompanied to the back of the sanctuary by the entire wedding party, so they can be ready to start the processional as soon as she is seated.

If a white carpet is used, it is unfurled by the ushers as soon as the mother of the bride has been seated. Late-arriving guests may be formally seated until the mother of the bride is seated; after that, the wedding has officially begun, and they must quickly take seats in the back of the sanctuary.

Considering how complicated much of this is, some special time should be set aside during the rehearsal to discuss the ushers' responsibilities.

At the end of the rehearsal, which is usually held at 5 or 6 P.M. and takes anywhere from fifteen minutes for an informal wedding (for which there also is often no rehearsal) to two hours, the wedding party heads to the rehearsal dinner. The party is festive and gay but shouldn't go on too late, as tomorrow is a very big day.

21
Your Wedding Day

FINALLY, the big day has arrived. No matter how excited you are, it is still a day to take with leisure, to enjoy, and to cherish for all its magic moments. If you have planned and organized carefully, there should be no last-minute worries to mar this special day.

Your hair and makeup should be perfect, your nails beautifully manicured. Your dress should be ready. After the final fitting, bring the dress to your house. Hang it on a high door, so the weight of the fabric will smooth out the wrinkles. Detach the train and hang it flat or place it on a large bed where it will rest undisturbed. If a touch-up is necessary, steam-press the dress on the wrong side. Should disaster strike, in the form of a lipstick or other kind of stain or a tear in the lace, call the shop or store where you bought the dress. They can best recommend how to repair the damage.

Have a leisurely breakfast before you start to dress. Now is the time to let your hospitality committee and your mother assume their responsibilities. The hospitality committee will function at the reception, and your mother will be sure everything is coming together to make your wedding day as smooth and beautiful as possible. She will oversee the photographer, caterer, and florist. On her wedding day, the bride has nothing to do but look lovely and enjoy herself.

As the hour of the wedding approaches, be sure to allow yourself enough time to prepare so the wedding can begin promptly on time. Many churches book several weddings on one day and the clergyperson's time is valuable, so it is a courtesy to everyone involved to make sure everything follows the time schedule that has been set up.

The best man will ride herd on the groom and the groomsmen, so you need not worry about that.

Your bridesmaids will have been told by you to report either to the church or to your home, and rides will have been arranged to get them where they are supposed to be. This is a task for which cousins and brothers come in handy. If there is a dressing room at the church, that may be the best place for all of you to dress.

When you leave for the church, be sure to take your dress and its accessories, a white lace-edged handkerchief, extra hose, facial tissue or white handkerchiefs for your bridesmaids and the mothers, a comb, makeup for touch-ups, and cologne. Tuck the beauty aids in a beaded or cloth evening purse. Spread a sheet over the car seat and floor to protect your dress. You should arrive at the church an hour in advance if you plan to dress there, even earlier if your bridal portrait will be taken there. If possible, bring a thermos of lemonade or some other refreshing drink and small sandwiches. In all the excitement of the day, some people may not have eaten enough, so the last-minute snack may forestall faintness during the ceremony.

As soon as you and your bridesmaids are dressed, the florist will show you how to carry your flowers. Pass out the handkerchiefs to your bridesmaids and mothers, but take a minute to remind everyone that this is a happy and joyous occasion and there is really no need for tears.

As you are making last-minute preparations, the guests will be arriving and the prelude music will be playing.

Some brides are willing to receive guests in the dressing room before the ceremony, while others are not. Mostly this depends upon the custom in your community. Sometimes the bride even goes out and mingles with the wedding guests before the wedding—especially if she is giving it. About ten or fifteen minutes prior to the hour set for the ceremony, everyone should make a last-minute check of their appearances and prepare to head to the sanctuary or room where the wedding will be held. There you will wait for the start of your wedding.

As your bridesmaids start down the aisle, take your father's arm and stand in position. When the music changes, take a deep breath and

step forward on your left foot to walk down the aisle to meet your waiting groom.

AFTER THE CEREMONY

As soon as you reach the back of the sanctuary, if wedding pictures will be taken while your guests head to the reception you and the wedding party should walk around to the door where the groom entered with the minister and wait there until all the guests have left the church. Then you can meet at the altar for portraits of the wedding party. The photographer should have been told that you want these pictures taken quickly so you do not keep your guests waiting too long. You may also have to meet with the clergyperson to sign and witness the marriage certificate, or you may have signed it before the ceremony. If the receiving line is formed at the back of the church, the pictures are taken immediately afterward.

THE RECEIVING LINE

If the reception is somewhere other than the church, immediately after the pictures are taken, the wedding party goes in prearranged transportation to the reception, where the receiving line is usually formed. After all the guests have gone through the receiving line, pictures may be taken of it. Guests always enjoy watching this, and it is more tactful to take these pictures after the receiving line than to keep guests waiting outside. Drinks should be served to guests as they walk away from the receiving line; a member of the hospitality committee can stand nearby and direct them to the refreshment table or bar.

The bride's mother, as official hostess, should always be the first person in the receiving line. If the bride has no mother, an aunt or grandmother serves as hostess. The fathers usually stand in line, or they may circulate among the guests. The bridesmaids are also optional to the receiving line. If they do stand in the line, they should position themselves after the maid or matron of honor. Either they all receive or no one does. The best man does not usually stand in the receiving line.

If there will be much delay between the time the ceremony is over and when the wedding party is able to arrive at the reception, have members of the hospitality committee speed to the reception site and offer drinks to waiting guests, who then go through the receiving line when you do arrive.

THE BRIDE'S TABLE

When there is a sit-down wedding breakfast, luncheon, or supper, seating at the bride's table is arranged in this way:

As a rule, only the bridal party is seated at the bride's table, although husbands and wives of attendants may be invited to sit at it, too, if there is room. The bride and groom sit next to each other—you on his right. Even if guests serve themselves at a buffet table, the bride's table is served by waiters or a serving committee. Place cards are necessary only on the bride's table and parents' table, but they may be used on

The receiving line (left to right): mother of the bride; father of the groom; mother of the groom; father of the bride; bride; groom; maid or matron of honor; bridesmaid; bridesmaid

The bride's table (left to right): usher; bridesmaid; best man; bride; groom; maid or matron of honor; usher; bridesmaid

all tables if a sit-down meal is served. The wedding cake is usually on a separate table.

At a stand-up reception it is thoughtful to have a few tables at the sides and in the corners for older people.

Your reception is a celebration in your honor, a lovely party. Although you and your groom are the guests of honor, you are, in a sense, also the host and hostess, and it is up to you to mingle with the guests and make them feel at home. Intimate family friends and relatives who have not already been invited are asked to drop by your parents' home if the party will continue there.

Enjoy yourself—this is one party at which you should and will, of course, have the time of your life.

THE PARENTS' TABLE

At a sit-down dinner, a parents' table is set up for both sets of parents. The clergyperson and his or her spouse, who must be invited to the reception but often decline to attend unless they know the bride and groom well, also sit here. The bride's father sits at the head of the table, with the groom's mother to his right. The bride's mother sits at the foot of the table with the groom's father to her right.

Though I am aware of the custom of arranging separate tables for each of the families, it does not particularly please me. I like to think that for one day, as two people start their new life, their families can intermingle and share one another's happiness.

TOASTS AT THE RECEPTION

The best man dons the mantle of master of ceremonies, offering the first toast, and then, in this order, calls upon the groom, the father of the groom, the father of the bride (and these days, also the mothers), and siblings who wish to offer toasts, and perhaps one or two others who can be counted on to offer something witty or warm. It is also up to the best man to be sure the toasting does not become drawn out or too sentimental.

All toasts may be, and perhaps are, best kept brief. The best man may say something as simple as, "To Jackie and Rusty, may they always be as happy as they are today." The groom usually toasts his bride's beauty, thanks her parents for making a lovely wedding possible, and he may also thank his parents for their support and warmth in welcoming his bride into the family. The groom's father offers a toast to the bride: "To our beautiful daughter-in-law, who doesn't need to be told how delighted we are to have her join our family." Then the bride's father toasts: "To our daughter and son-in-law; may you always be happy."

After the toasts, the best man reads any telegrams that have been sent by persons who could not attend.

Sometimes this ceremonial work of the best man is taken over by a professional master of ceremonies, usually the bandleader or the caterer. When this happens, more often than not, my worst fears usually come true as I watch the entire reception become overblown. Guests are herded about, small traditions such as tossing the bride's garter or bouquet become overorchestrated and awkward. The sad result is a great loss of spontaneity. Steps can be taken to prevent this happening at your wedding. You can tell the best man that you would like him to offer the toasts and make any announcements, and then tell the bandleader that you have asked the best man to do this. Or you can tell the bandleader that you would like announcements kept to the minimum, and even give him or her a list of what you want announced.

It is kind, however, to announce when you are about to cut the cake or throw your garter or bouquet. That way, all your guests will feel like part of the party and they will know what is going on.

THE WEDDING CAKE

The cutting of the wedding cake is always a highlight of the reception. The guests are signaled by a fanfare or by the clinking of a glass by the best man. Usually a silver cake knife with a beribboned handle is used. The groom places his hand over your hand on the knife handle, and together, you cut the first slice, which is shared by you as a symbol of your willingness to share each other's lives.

After the first ceremonial piece is cut, someone usually steps in to complete the cutting.

DANCING

When there is dancing at a reception, by tradition the bride and groom dance the first dance alone for a minute or two. Then the bride's father cuts in on the groom to dance with his daughter, and the groom dances with the bride's mother. Fourth, the groom's parents come to the floor, and the groom's father dances with the bride. Fifth, the bride's father cuts in on the groom and dances with the bride's mother. Sixth, the groom dances with his mother. Seventh, the bride's parents exchange dances with the groom's parents. Eighth, the best man dances with the bride. Ninth, the groom dances with the maid of honor. Finally the wedding party—bridesmaids and ushers—join on the dance floor. If all this sounds confusing, it isn't. The order of the dancing will make more sense to you if you read it through a couple of times—and besides, if someone errs, it doesn't matter anyway. By the way, especially if the wedding party is formally dressed, a waltz is lovely for this

dance. When the whole wedding party is on the dance floor, the other guests join in.

THE GUEST-BOOK TABLE

Years later, you will be grateful if you asked those attending your wedding to sign a guest book as they entered the reception. A special book can be purchased in a gift or stationery store; bridal shops also sometimes carry them.

Ask a friend who's willing to help out by standing next to the table as people arrive and asking them to sign.

The guest-book table is set up near the door, so guests can sign it after they remove their coats. Cover the table with a white or pastel cloth and put a small bouquet on it. It is a nice touch to have a pretty, beribboned pen for people to use.

TOSSING YOUR BOUQUET AND GARTER

Your bouquet and garter are usually tossed shortly before you leave to change into street clothes so you and your new husband can leave the reception. Someone you designate or the bandleader, if he or she is master of ceremonies, should gather the wedding party for these small ceremonies. Other single men and women can also participate.

LEAVING THE RECEPTION

Most receptions last two and a half to four hours. Some guests may leave before the bride and groom. Many, though, will want to stay to see you off, so you should be aware of this and plan your exit accordingly.

As noted, the reception comes to a close when you throw your bouquet and garter and leave to change clothes. Traditionally, the bride and groom change in separate rooms. As a thoughtful bride, you may want to call your mother and father into your changing room to thank them one more time for giving you such a lovely wedding. Certainly, you and your groom should seek out both sets of parents to tell them good-bye.

The remaining wedding guests traditionally throw rice (which, contrary to popular myth, does not hurt birds) after a departing bride and groom, although some couples prefer bird seed (which is helpful to birds) or flower petals (which are expensive). Whatever you decide, wrap small packets in tulle and tie them with pretty ribbons, leaving a basket near the exit for guests to use.

Finally, although there will be much joking and great interest in where you are spending the night, a savvy bride and groom reveal this to no one. The public part of your wedding ends when you leave the reception, and the private part is just for the two of you.

22
Calling It Off

ALTHOUGH every couple will have some doubts and last-minute jitters, most go through with the wedding. Knowing that a mild case of nerves is perfectly normal, however, shouldn't stop either person from calling off the wedding if serious doubts exist.

A broken engagement is painful for everyone involved, but it is far less painful than an unhappy marriage. If the engagement has not been formally announced, you can simply pass the word to a few close friends who will tell other people. A detailed explanation is not required—indeed, none is necessary—and tactful friends will not press for one. You need only say that you have broken up. Why you have made such a decision is strictly your own business.

If the engagement has been formally announced in the papers, a brief announcement to the effect that it is now broken is in order. It usually reads:

Mr. and Mrs. Bruce Long Jones announce that the engagement of their daughter Jane Ann and Mr. George James Adams has been ended by mutual consent.

If the wedding invitations have been sent, a printed announcement must be prepared and mailed as soon as possible, if there is time before the wedding. (If there is no time, the announcement must be made by telegram and telephone.) A formal announcement could be worded as follows:

Mr. and Mrs. Bruce Long Jones

announce that the marriage of their daughter

Jane Ann

to

Mr. George James Adams

will not take place

A telegram could be worded: "The marriage of our daughter Jane Ann to Mr. George James Adams will not take place. Mr. and Mrs. Bruce Long Jones."

As soon as the wedding is called off, notify all suppliers, such as the baker, the florist, and the photographer; also notify the clergyperson and others involved.

Occasionally a wedding is postponed, due to illness on the part of the bride, groom, or a close family member. Guests may be telephoned or sent telegrams if time is short, or, if there is time, a printed announcement may be sent. It should read:

Mr. and Mrs. Bryan Miller
announce that the marriage of their daughter
Carrie Elizabeth

to

David Burns
has been postponed from
Saturday, the sixteenth of June

until

Saturday, the twentieth of August
at two-thirty o'clock
St. Elygius Church
Chicago

When there is a death in the family, a large wedding may be postponed, in which case the above announcement is sent. A large wedding that is postponed due to a death in the family may still take place privately before the immediate family. Under such circumstances, the announcement would read:

> Mr. and Mrs. Marshall Stock
> regret that they are obliged to recall
> the invitation to the marriage of their daughter
> Andrea Sue
>
> to
>
> John Park Stone
> owing to the death of Mr. Stone's father
> Mr. Harold Travers Stone

To this can be added the following lines:

> The ceremony will be held privately
> in the presence of the immediate family.

23
Now That You're Married

USING YOUR NEW NAME

YOU were Jacqueline Marie Young before your marriage. You married John Anthony Gray. Assuming you change your name, Mrs. John Anthony Gray becomes your formal married name. It is the name you have engraved on informal note cards and your calling card.

A growing trend exists among young women to keep their own names after marriage either professionally or in all facets of their lives. If this is your choice, the first step is to check the legal requirements of the state you reside in to see if you must do anything to keep your maiden name. In most states, the answer is no. If you have decided to keep your own name, you will probably want to tell friends informally and to include this fact in newspaper announcements of your wedding. Some women report having some difficulty in retaining their own names. This is because it has not yet become the norm throughout the country, and many people—your great-aunt Bessie, for one—may resist it. At the same time that you make a decision to keep your own name, you must also decide how much you are going to insist on it. One woman I know who had established herself professionally and married at a relatively late age felt adamant about using her own name, but decided that she would not press this upon certain people. Her husband takes pride in introducing her by her own name, and she uses it routinely with all new acquaintances and diligently reminds old friends, but does not harp

186

on it to other people—like her traditional mother—for whom the use of her new name is akin to a political cause.

STATIONERY

If you continue to use your name, your stationery is printed just as it always has been. If you use your husband's name, your personal stationery should be printed with your first name, your maiden name or middle name if you want to use it, and your new surname. It should not be printed *Mrs. William Wiley;* that is reserved for informal (fold-over) notes and calling cards. (Although calling cards are not used for formal calls anymore, I still think they make excellent gift enclosures and are useful for certain kinds of invitations, and I recommend them. These can be printed with your name alone or with *Mr. and Mrs. John Jones.*)

When you do not change your name, ordering joint stationery presents more problems. I cannot think of a graceful way for an informal note or a calling card to be printed with both your names. Some people have informals and other stationery printed with first names only, but I think this is too casual. Another solution, one that appeals to many independent-minded couples, is for each to keep his or her separate writing paper. Perhaps you can work with a good typographer to design a letterhead that you can both use. Another solution is to design a joint monogram using both your surnames and use that on all stationery. For example:

F ⫟ W

ABOUT MONOGRAMS

The use of a monogram on luggage, linens, and clothes is an old bridal tradition that is not much used today. Such monograms use the first initial of your first name, the initial of your maiden name, and the first

initial of your husband's surname. On silver and as a second choice
for linens, the initial of your husband's surname is preferred.

SIGNING LETTERS

If you don't change your name, you won't have to worry about your
new signature. Should you elect to call yourself Mrs. John Anthony
Gray, you still almost never sign anything *Mrs. John Anthony Gray.* Use
your name, Jacqueline Gray, in whatever form you choose, on legal
papers, checks, and letters. Only on business correspondence relating
to your household will you sign *Mrs. John Anthony Gray* in parentheses
under or to the left of your signature or typed name.

IN PUBLIC

In public places and by those who serve you, you will be addressed
as "Mrs. Jones." If you are keeping your own name, you do not
become "Mrs." at all, but rather continue to be referred to as "Miss
Smith," or "Ms. Smith." Some women, particularly after they have
children, begin to use their husbands' names socially even if they
retain their own names professionally.

INTRODUCING EACH OTHER

Husbands and wives do not refer to each other during introductions
as "Mr. Gray" or "Mrs. Gray." Nor should a man refer to his wife as
"the missus," "the wife," or "the better half." Simply say, "May I
introduce my husband," or "This is my wife." If the woman has kept
her own name, the man may want to repeat it when introducing her
to a stranger.

AND FINALLY . . .

You are officially newlyweds for one year after you marry, which basically means that others do not expect too much of you, particularly in terms of entertaining. This is a time to treasure one another, get used to living together, enjoy your time alone, and, in general, take the time you need to settle into your new life.

Having said all this, however, I want to suggest that, although this is not required, one of the loveliest gestures of appreciation you can make toward everyone who helped to make your wedding successful is to make sure they are among the first guests invited to your new home. Your attendants will have been entertained in connection with your wedding, so I am really speaking of those who served as your hospitality committee, the aunt who acted as a behind-the-scenes major domo at the reception, and any other personal friends who contributed in some special way to your wonderful day. You will be loved for this extra special touch of thoughtfulness.

BRIDE'S ORGANIZER

OUR ENGAGEMENT ANNOUNCEMENT

Our Wedding Traditions

The weather on our wedding day was _____
_____

Wedding ring traditions _____
_____

Something old _____
Something new _____
Something borrowed _____
Something blue _____
And a lucky sixpence in your shoe! _____
_____

My bouquet was caught by _____
My garter was caught by _____
I was given away by _____
Showers were given by _____

        on _____

        at _____

        by _____

        on _____

        at _____

The cake surprise went to _____
The bachelor party took place on _____

        at _____

Other traditions _____
_____
_____
_____
_____
_____
_____
_____

Cost Estimates for Wedding and Reception Services

	First Bid	Second Bid	Actual Cost
Reception Site			
Church	$____	$____	$____
Banquet room of hotel or restaurant	$____	$____	$____
Private club	$____	$____	$____
Other	$____	$____	$____
Total	$____	$____	$____
Printing			
Invitations	$____	$____	$____
Reception cards	$____	$____	$____
Announcements	$____	$____	$____
At-home cards	$____	$____	$____
Informals	$____	$____	$____
Thank-you cards	$____	$____	$____
Reception napkins	$____	$____	$____
Matches	$____	$____	$____
Cake boxes	$____	$____	$____
Extras	$____	$____	$____
Total	$____	$____	$____
Flowers			
Wedding			
Church, home, hotel, etc.	$____	$____	$____
Bouquets	$____	$____	$____
Corsages	$____	$____	$____
Boutonnieres	$____	$____	$____
Total	$____	$____	$____
Reception			
Receiving line	$____	$____	$____
Buffet centerpieces	$____	$____	$____
Table decorations	$____	$____	$____
Cake table	$____	$____	$____
Guest-book table	$____	$____	$____
Total	$____	$____	$____

Cost Estimates for Wedding and Reception Services (*cont.*)

	First Bid	Second Bid	Actual Cost
Wedding Attire			
Wedding gown	$____	$____	$____
Veil	$____	$____	$____
Accessories	$____	$____	$____
Trousseau	$____	$____	$____
Total	$____	$____	$____
Photography			
Engagement portrait	$____	$____	$____
Wedding portrait	$____	$____	$____
Candids	$____	$____	$____
Duplicate prints for groom's parents, attendants, etc.	$____	$____	$____
Total	$____	$____	$____
Music			
Wedding	$____	$____	$____
Reception	$____	$____	$____
Rehearsal	$____	$____	$____
Rehearsal dinner	$____	$____	$____
Total	$____	$____	$____
Food, Beverages, and Service			
Bridal Luncheon	$____	$____	$____
Rehearsal Dinner	$____	$____	$____
Reception			
Food	$____	$____	$____
Liquor	$____	$____	$____
Nonalcoholic beverages	$____	$____	$____
Wedding cake	$____	$____	$____
Service (waiters, bartenders, etc.)	$____	$____	$____
Total	$____	$____	$____

Cost Estimates for Wedding and Reception Services (*cont.*)

	First Bid	Second Bid	Actual Cost
Donations			
Church			$___
Minister			$___
Sexton			$___
Organist	$___	$___	$___
Janitors at church			$___
Wedding consultant at church			$___
Police officer in charge of traffic and			
parking in front of church			$___
Total $___			
Gifts			
Attendants	$___	$___	$___
Groom	$___	$___	$___
Wedding ring for groom	$___	$___	$___
Total $___	$___	$___	
Transportation	$___	$___	$___
Miscellaneous			
Table favors	$___	$___	$___
Candles	$___	$___	$___
Hotel accommodations	$___	$___	$___
Prerehearsal party	$___	$___	$___
Mother's gown and accessories	$___	$___	$___
Father's outfit and accessories	$___	$___	$___
Others	$___	$___	$___
Total $___	$___	$___	
Total Wedding Cost	$___	$___	$___

Important Names, Addresses, and Appointments

Person in charge of wedding site _____ Phone _____

Address _____ Appt. _____

Clergy or ceremony official _____ Phone _____

Address _____ Appt. _____

Church wedding consultant _____ Phone _____

Address _____ Appt. _____

Organist _____ Phone _____

Address _____ Appt. _____

Soloist _____ Phone _____

Address _____ Appt. _____

Printer/stationer _____ Phone _____

Address _____ Appt. _____

Florist _____ Phone _____

Address _____ Appt. _____

Baker _____ Phone _____

Address _____ Appt. _____

Photographer _____ Phone _____

Address _____ Appt. _____

Travel agent _____ Phone _____

Address _____ Appt. _____

Doctor _____ Phone _____

Address _____ Appt. _____

Jeweler _____ Phone _____

Address _____ Appt. _____

Bridal consultant _____ Store _____ Phone _____

Address _____ Appt. _____

Bridal consultant _____ Store _____ Phone _____

Address _____ Appt. _____

Important Names, Addresses, and Appointments (*cont.*)

Bridal consultant _____ Store _____ Phone _____

Address _____ Appt. _____

Bridal consultant _____ Store _____ Phone _____

Address _____ Appt. _____

**Seamstress for bride's, attendants', and
   flower girl's gowns** _____ Phone _____

Address _____ Appt. _____

Hairdresser _____ Phone _____

Address _____ Appt. _____

Limousine service _____ Phone _____

Address _____ Appt. _____

**Manager of hotel where out-of-town
   guests will stay** _____ Phone _____

Address _____ Appt. _____

Person in charge of reception site _____ Phone _____

Address _____ Appt. _____

Caterer _____ Phone _____

Address _____ Appt. _____

Musicians for reception _____ Phone _____

Address _____ Appt. _____

Others _____ Phone _____

Address _____ Appt. _____

Others _____ Phone _____

Address _____ Appt. _____

Others _____ Phone _____

Address _____ Appt. _____

Others _____ Phone _____

Address _____ Appt. _____

Transportation Checklist

Drivers to church and to reception

Bride to church with father (or father and mother):
Driver _____ Phone _____
Time to be at house _____

Bridesmaids to church and return for reception:
Driver _____ Phone _____ Time _____
Bridesmaid's address _____ Phone _____
Driver _____ Phone _____ Time _____
Bridesmaid's address _____ Phone _____
Driver _____ Phone _____ Time _____
Bridesmaid's address _____ Phone _____
Driver _____ Phone _____ Time _____
Bridesmaid's address _____ Phone _____
Driver _____ Phone _____ Time _____
Bridesmaid's address _____ Phone _____

Bride's mother, unless she rides with bride or bridesmaids:
Driver _____ Phone _____ Time _____
Bride's parents' address _____ Phone _____
Driver _____ Phone _____ Time _____

Bride's grandparents:
Driver _____ Phone _____ Time _____

Groom's parents:
Driver _____ Phone _____ Time _____
Address _____

Groom's grandparents' address _____ Phone _____
Driver _____ Phone _____ Time _____

Bride and groom to reception:
Driver _____ Phone _____

Transportation Checklist for Out-of-Town Guests

ARRIVING

Date	Person to be met	Place	Time	Address to be taken to	Person responsible

Transportation Checklist for Out-of-Town Guests (*cont.*)

DEPARTING

Date	Person to be met	Place	Time	Address to be taken to	Person responsible

Sample Form for Wedding Announcement

To: *Society Editor*   For *Release:* _____

Full name of bride _____

Full name of bride's parents _____

Address _____ Phone _____

Bride's schools _____ When? _____

Bride's affiliations _____

Full name of bridegroom _____

Full name of bridegroom's parents _____

Address _____ Phone _____

Bridegroom's schools _____ When? _____

Bridegroom's affiliations _____

Wedding date and time _____

Wedding place _____

Reception place _____

Honeymoon _____

Future home _____

Bride's honor attendants _____ Best Man _____

_____ Ushers _____

Her other attendants _____

_____

_____ Clergyperson _____

Person giving bride in marriage _____

Bride's gown _____

_____

Veil _____ Bouquet _____

Attendants' costumes _____

_____ Flowers _____

Decorations at church _____

Decorations at reception _____

Bride's mother's costume _____

Bridegroom's mother's costume _____

Going-away costume _____

_____

Out-of-town guests were from _____

Our Wedding Party

Maid (or Matron) of Honor _____ Phone _____
Address _____
Dress size _____ Bust _____ Waist _____ Hips _____
Sleeve (shoulder to wrist) _____ Neck _____ Head _____
Length (waist to floor) _____ Glove size _____ Shoe size _____

Bridesmaid _____ Phone _____
Address _____
Dress size _____ Bust _____ Waist _____ Hips _____
Sleeve (shoulder to wrist) _____ Neck _____ Head _____
Length (waist to floor) _____ Glove size _____ Shoe size _____

Bridesmaid _____ Phone _____
Address _____
Dress size _____ Bust _____ Waist _____ Hips _____
Sleeve (shoulder to wrist) _____ Neck _____ Head _____
Length (waist to floor) _____ Glove size _____ Shoe size _____

Bridesmaid _____ Phone _____
Address _____
Dress size _____ Bust _____ Waist _____ Hips _____
Sleeve (shoulder to wrist) _____ Neck _____ Head _____
Length (waist to floor) _____ Glove size _____ Shoe size _____

Bridesmaid _____ Phone _____
Address _____
Dress size _____ Bust _____ Waist _____ Hips _____
Sleeve (shoulder to wrist) _____ Neck _____ Head _____
Length (waist to floor) _____ Glove size _____ Shoe size _____

Bridesmaid _____ Phone _____
Address _____
Dress size _____ Bust _____ Waist _____ Hips _____
Sleeve (shoulder to wrist) _____ Neck _____ Head _____
Length (waist to floor) _____ Glove size _____ Shoe size _____

Our Wedding Party (*cont.*)

Bridesmaid _____ Phone _____
Address _____
Dress size _____ Bust _____ Waist _____ Hips _____
Sleeve (shoulder to wrist) _____ Neck _____ Head _____
Length (waist to floor) _____ Glove size _____ Shoe size _____

Bridesmaid _____ Phone _____
Address _____
Dress size _____ Bust _____ Waist _____ Hips _____
Sleeve (shoulder to wrist) _____ Neck _____ Head _____
Length (waist to floor) _____ Glove size _____ Shoe size _____

Bridesmaid _____ Phone _____
Address _____
Dress size _____ Bust _____ Waist _____ Hips _____
Sleeve (shoulder to wrist) _____ Neck _____ Head _____
Length (waist to floor) _____ Glove size _____ Shoe size _____

Best Man _____ Phone _____
Address _____
Waist _____ Inseam _____ Shoe size _____
Glove size _____ Jacket size _____ Shirt size _____

Usher _____ Phone _____
Address _____
Waist _____ Inseam _____ Shoe size _____
Glove size _____ Jacket size _____ Shirt size _____

Usher _____ Phone _____
Address _____
Waist _____ Inseam _____ Shoe size _____
Glove size _____ Jacket size _____ Shirt size _____

Usher _____ Phone _____
Address _____
Waist _____ Inseam _____ Shoe size _____
Glove size _____ Jacket size _____ Shirt size _____

Our Wedding Party (*cont.*)

Usher _____ Phone _____
Address _____
Waist _____ Inseam _____ Shoe size _____
Glove size _____ Jacket size _____ Shirt size _____

Usher _____ Phone _____
Address _____
Waist _____ Inseam _____ Shoe size _____
Glove size _____ Jacket size _____ Shirt size _____

Usher _____ Phone _____
Address _____
Waist _____ Inseam _____ Shoe size _____
Glove size _____ Jacket size _____ Shirt size _____

Usher _____ Phone _____
Address _____
Waist _____ Inseam _____ Shoe size _____
Glove size _____ Jacket size _____ Shirt size _____

Usher _____ Phone _____
Address _____
Waist _____ Inseam _____ Shoe size _____
Glove size _____ Jacket size _____ Shirt size _____

Usher _____ Phone _____
Address _____
Waist _____ Inseam _____ Shoe size _____
Glove size _____ Jacket size _____ Shirt size _____

Usher _____ Phone _____
Address _____
Waist _____ Inseam _____ Shoe size _____
Glove size _____ Jacket size _____ Shirt size _____

Usher _____ Phone _____
Address _____
Waist _____ Inseam _____ Shoe size _____
Glove size _____ Jacket size _____ Shirt size _____

Our Wedding Party (*cont.*)

Flower girl _____ Phone _____
Address _____
Dress size _____ Bust _____ Waist _____ Hips _____
Sleeve (shoulder to wrist) _____ Neck _____ Head _____
Length (waist to floor) _____ Glove size _____ Shoe size _____

Ring bearer _____ Phone _____
Address _____
Waist _____ Inseam _____ Shoe size _____
Glove size _____ Jacket size _____ Shirt size _____

Special attendant _____ Phone _____
Address _____

Special attendant _____ Phone _____
Address _____

Special attendant _____ Phone _____
Address _____

Special attendant _____ Phone _____
Address _____

Overall supervisor _____ Phone _____
Address _____

Groom's parents _____ Phone _____
Address _____
_____ Phone _____
Address _____

Our Wedding Ceremony Music

(Copies to be given to all musicians and soloists)

Prelude selections (to begin _____ minutes before the ceremony):

_____

_____

_____

_____

_____

_____

First solo (to be sung _____ minutes before the ceremony):

_____

Second solo (to be sung _____ minutes before the ceremony):

_____

Processional (to be played after bride's mother is seated):

_____

Music to be played during ceremony (optional):

_____

_____

Recessional _____

_____

_____

Name of soloist _____ Phone _____

Address _____ Fee _____

Name of musician _____ Phone _____

Address _____ Fee _____

Florist's Information Sheet

(Copy to be given to florist)

Name of bride _____ Phone _____

Address _____

Ceremony date _____ Time _____ Location _____
_____

Reception time _____ Location _____
_____

Color and type of wedding dress _____
Color, size, and type of bridal bouquet _____
_____ Ribbon color _____ Cost _____
Color and type of corsage for bride's going-away costume _____
_____ Cost _____
Bride's mother _____
   Color of dress _____ Type of corsage _____ Cost _____
   Corsage to be sent to _____ Date _____ Time _____
Groom's mother _____
   Color of dress _____ Type of corsage _____ Cost _____
   Corsage to be sent to _____ Date _____ Time _____
Bride's grandmother(s) _____
   Type of corsage _____ Cost _____
   Corsage to be sent to _____ Date _____ Time _____
   _____ Date _____ Time _____
Groom's grandmother(s) _____
   Type of corsage _____ Cost _____
   Corsage to be sent to _____ Date _____ Time _____
   _____ Date _____ Time _____
Material sample of bridesmaids' dresses

Material sample of flower girl's dress

Color, size, and type of attendants' bouquets _____
_____ Ribbon color _____ Cost _____

Florist Information Sheet (*cont.*)

Style and type of flowers for floral headdresses, if these are being used
_____ Cost _____
Amount and type of petals or flowers for flower girl's basket _____
_____ Cost _____
Bridal bouquet and all attendants' flowers to be delivered to _____
_____
  Date_____Time_____

Number and type of boutonnieres desired for the groom, best man,
  ushers, and fathers _____ Cost _____
  Boutonnieres to be delivered to _____
  Date _____ Time _____

Names and addresses of relatives, friends, organist, soloist, reception
  servers, and others who are to be sent corsages; color and type of
  corsages to be sent; date and time to be sent: Cost _____

1. _____   2. _____
   _____   _____
   _____   _____
   Date _____ Time _____   Date _____ Time _____
3. _____   4. _____
   _____   _____
   _____   _____
   Date _____ Time _____   Date _____ Time _____

Church Decorations

Cushion to be supplied for ring bearer: Yes _____ No _____ Cost _____
Aisle carpet: Yes _____ No _____ Cost _____
Type and color of flowers to be used in church decorations _____
_____
_____Cost _____
Number of aisles to be decorated _____
Type and color of flowers to be used in aisle decorations _____
_____
_____Cost _____
Aisle ribbons to be used: Yes _____ No _____ Cost _____
All church flowers and decorations to be delivered to _____
_____ Date _____ Time _____
Person to contact at church for additional information _____
_____ Phone _____

Reception Decorations

Type and color of flowers to be used for the reception decorations:
Receiving line background _____
_____Cost _____
Centerpieces:
　　Bride's table _____ Cost _____
　　Parents' table _____ Cost _____
　　Buffet tables: How many _____
　　　　　　　　Type and color _____ Cost _____
　　Guests' tables: How many _____
　　　　　　　　Type and color _____ Cost _____
　　Guest-book table _____ Cost _____
　　Wedding-cake table _____ Cost _____
White satin ribbons and flowers secured on wedding knife: Yes ___
No _____ Cost _____
Small flowers with white satin ribbons tied to stems of champagne
toast glasses: Yes _____ No _____ Cost _____
Greens and fresh red rose petals to surround wedding cake: Yes ___
No _____ Cost _____
All reception flowers and bride's going-away corsage to be delivered
to _____Date _____ Time _____
Person to contact at reception site for additional information _____
_____ Phone _____

Bridal Luncheon Decorations

Type and color of flowers _____
_____Cost _____
Flowers to be delivered to _____
　　Date _____ Time _____

Rehearsal Dinner Decorations

Type and color of flowers _____
_____ Cost _____
Number of centerpieces _____ Cost _____
Flowers to be delivered to _____
　　Date _____ Time _____

Flowers for After the Wedding

Type and color of thank-you flowers for mothers, friends, and relatives who helped with wedding _____
_____ Cost _____
Where and when to deliver:

1. _____
_____
_____

Date _____

2. _____
_____
_____

Date _____

3. _____
_____
_____

Date _____

4. _____
_____
_____

Date _____

Transporting Wedding Presents

Who: _____
_____
_____

When & Where to deliver: _____
_____
_____

Musical Organization for the Reception

(Copy to be given to musicians)

Name of bride _____ Phone _____
Address _____
Reception date _____ Time _____
Location _____
Time of arrival for musicians _____ Cost _____
Music to begin as first guests arrive (light, joyous music) _____
_____

Music to be played as wedding party arrives _____
_____

Music to be played as guests go through receiving line (old standards
are "When I Fall in Love," "It Had to Be You," "I'll Be Loving You
Always," "Autumn Leaves") _____
_____
_____

Music to be played as wedding party sits down to eat (your favorite
songs) _____
_____

Music to be played for the first dance
    1. Bride and groom ("The Girl That I Marry") _____
    _____

    2. Father and bride ("Thank Heaven for Little Girls") _____
    _____

    3. Groom with mother of bride ("I Want a Girl Just Like the Girl
       That Married Dear Old Dad") _____
    4. Groom's Father with Bride ("True Love") _____
    5. Bride's Father with Bride's Mother ("When I Fall in Love") ___

Other music to be played _____
_____
_____

Music to be played as fanfares (watch _____ for signals)
    During cake-cutting _____
    As bride tosses her bouquet _____
    As groom throws bride's garter _____
    As bride and groom leave the reception _____

Beverages for the Reception

*(Copies to be given to the liquor merchant and
person in charge of the reception)*

Name of bride _____ Phone _____
Address _____
Reception date _____ Time _____
Location _____
Number of guests _____

Gin . . . . Brand _____ Quantity _____
Vermouth . . . . Brand _____ Quantity _____
Bonded bourbon . . . . Brand _____ Quantity _____
Straight whiskey . . . . Brand _____ Quantity _____
Scotch . . . . Brand _____ Quantity _____
Vodka . . . . Brand _____ Quantity _____
Other . . . . Brand _____ Quantity _____
Other . . . . Brand _____ Quantity _____
Champagne . . . . Brand _____ Quantity _____
Other wines . . . . Brand _____ Quantity _____
                                   Brand _____ Quantity _____

Punch (with champagne) _____
Punch (plain) _____
Mixers

    Ginger ale _____
    Bitter lemon _____
    Tonic _____
    Club soda _____
    Cola _____
    Noncola _____
    Lemon juice _____
    Pineapple juice (unsweetened) _____
    Orange juice _____
    Tomato juice _____

Beverages for the Reception (*cont.*)

*(Copies to be given to the liquor merchant and
person in charge of the reception)*

Limes _____

Lemons _____

Oranges _____

Onions _____

Maraschino cherries _____

Ice _____

Equipment
   Champagne, cocktail, and tall 8-ounce glasses (no plastic)

_____

Bottle openers _____

Pitchers _____

Knives _____

Large buckets for icing champagne _____

Small champagne buckets for bride's and parents' tables_____

Ice tongs _____

Cocktail shakers _____

Ice buckets _____

Swizzle sticks _____

Cleaning cloths _____

Napkins _____

Total cost of all beverages and equipment _____

(It's a good idea to have liquor merchant sign an agreement regarding
total cost.)

Prewedding Festivities

Engagement Party

Date _____ Time _____ Location _____

Host or hostess _____

Bridal Showers

Date _____ Time _____ Location _____

Type of shower _____
Host or hostess
Date _____ Time _____ Location _____

Type of shower _____
Host or hostess _____

Bride's Luncheon

Date _____ Time _____ Location _____

Host or hostess (if not given by bride) _____

Bachelor Party

Date _____ Time _____ Location _____

Host (if not given by groom) _____

Parties of Out-of-Town Guests

Date _____ Time _____ Location _____

Host or hostess _____
Date _____ Time _____ Location _____

Host or hostess _____

Rehearsal Dinner

Date _____ Time _____ Location _____

_____

HOUSEHOLD ORGANIZER

THE following pages list the items you need (or may simply want) to set up a household. These lists will also help you plan for the bridal registry.

I've made suggestions about quantities where appropriate. Not too many years ago, no bride's household was complete without twelve place settings of china and sterling. Because today's households are often smaller and less complicated than those of a generation ago, I and most other experts now recommend eight place settings. I would even go one step further and say that if you know your entertaining will be infrequent and casual, then you might want to dispense with the china and sterling altogether and put your money into some wonderful casual dishes and stainless flatware. Of course, such decisions can be based only on what you perceive your needs to be.

In other places where I've mentioned quantity, I've listed the minimum to run a two-person household. As for furniture, I've described the basics that are required to set up a new household. You may want or need more.

DISHES, GLASSWARE, FLATWARE

China and Everyday Dishes

8 5-piece place settings (each place setting consisting of a dinner plate, salad plate, bowl, cup and saucer) in china and everyday dishes

6–8 extra salad/dessert plates

8–12 mugs

Serving pieces:

Vegetable dishes

Gravy boat

Sauce dishes

Sugar bowl

Creamer

Platters

Bowls

Coffee pot

Teapot

Glassware

Crystal or suitable for entertaining:

8 all-purpose wineglasses

8 water goblets

8–24 champagne glasses

8–24 beer glasses

Everyday glasses:

> 8 large tumblers
>
> 8 medium tumblers
>
> 8 juice glasses

Nice to have:

Sets (4–8 or more) specialized liqueur glasses: sherry, cognac, etc.

Pitchers

Punch bowl and serving cups

Dessert goblets

Compotes

Candlesticks

Flatware

> 8 5-piece place settings (each place setting consisting of 1 dinner fork, 1 dinner knife, 1 dinner spoon, 1 salad fork, 1 teaspoon), silver or silver plate
>
> 8 5-piece place settings of stainless steak knives

Serving pieces:

Forks

Spoons (regular and pierced)

Cake knife/pie server

Gravy ladle

Meat-carving set

Salad fork and spoon

Nice to have:

Serving trays and platters

Serving dishes

Candlesticks/candelabra

Salt and pepper shakers

Creamer/sugar bowl

Pitchers

Gravy boat

KITCHEN

Basic Cookware

Saucepans, 1 quart and 2 quart

Skillets, 8 inch and 10 inch

Double boiler

Dutch oven

Soup pot

Roasting pan

Broiling pan

Tea kettle

Casseroles, 1 quart, 2 quart, 4 quart

Cake pans

Pie plates

Cookie sheets

Mixing bowls

Basic Appliances

Microwave oven

Toaster oven

Electric mixer

Food processer

Waffle iron

Electric can opener

Blender

Toaster

Nice to have:

Coffee grinder

Mini food processor

Espresso maker

Ice-cream maker

Electric whisks

Juice extractor

Pressure cooker

Wok

Fish poacher

Muffin tins, molds, ramekins, custard cups

Basic Utensils

Utensil set (spatula, slotted spoon, etc.)

Wooden spoons

Wire whisks

Measuring cups and spoons

Cutting board

Grater

Garlic press

Bulb baster

Colander/strainers

Corkscrew

Set of knives

Knife sharpener

Vegetable peeler

Salt and pepper mills

Kitchen shears

Vegetable steamer

Rolling pin

Pastry brush

Pastry blender

Flour sifter

Timer

Food-storage containers

Dish drainer

Nice to have:

Pastry bag and attachments

Melon-ball scoop

Apple corer

Poultry shears

Marble pastry slab

Cookie cutters

LINENS

Kitchen

2 pot holders

4 terry-cloth dish towels

12 glass towels

Dining

2 tablecloths (1 formal, 1 informal)

8 napkins for each tablecloth

Bath

2 bath sets per person (large towel or bath sheet, 1 hand towel, 1 washcloth)

2 bath mats

Shower curtain

Rug

Lid-cover set

Bedroom

2 sets of sheets and pillow cases for each bed

2 blankets for each bed (1 summer weight; 1 winter weight)

Pillows

Comforter

Bedspreads

Nice to have:

2–4 sets guest towels

HOUSEWARES

Vacuum cleaner

Electric broom

Mops, including dust mop

Broom and dustpan

Ironing board and iron

Laundry hamper

Wastebaskets (1 per room)

Garbage pail(s)

Tool kit

Sewing machine

Sewing kit

Bathroom scale

BASIC FURNITURE

Living Room

Sofa

Chairs

Coffee table

End tables

Lamps

Television/stereo

TV/stereo storage unit

Floor covering

Window treatment (curtains, blinds, etc.)

Bedroom

Bed

Dressers

Night tables

Lamps

Chair

Floor covering

Window treatment (curtain, blinds, etc.)

Dining Room

Table

Chairs

Floor covering

Window treatment

Creature comforts

Pictures

Mirrors

Clocks

Tray tables

Desk

Bookcases

Sconces

Shelves

SPECIAL TIPS FROM RECENT BRIDES

Recent brides from across the country contributed these suggestions, along with many others we just didn't have room for, to help you make your day—and the planning leading up to it—go as smoothly and beautifully as you wish. Some of these tips are ideas you'll want to share with your fiancé and the others who are helping you plan your wedding; others are just for you.

☐ If your parents live far away, keep them posted on the wedding plans via the internet. If they don't have a computer and an e-mail account, set one up for them at the local library. They won't want to miss out on the plans, and this is much faster than sending pictures by mail.

☐ When planning your ceremony and reception, it's nice to ask friends and family if they'd like to participate. If your cousin's a gifted violinist, your friend is a wiz at computer graphics or videotaping, or your aunt loves to do calligraphy, you just might end up with homemade, personalized elements that add another dimension to your day, create a special role for them, and save money, too.

☐ Keep in mind that many reception halls get booked early—one to two years in advance in many cases. Don't rely on verbal agreements; get everything in writing, down to details such as the caterer's access to the kitchen, the linens which will be used, closing time, etc. No detail is too small to consider in advance.

☐ While shopping for your dress, keep in mind you'll need to pick up the following items. Even if you don't see the dress of your dreams at the first few stores you visit, you can keep an eye out for these: Shoes, handbag, stockings, lingerie (bustier/ bra, panties), slip/crinoline, headpiece/veil, handkerchief, garter, gloves, wrap/cape, necklace and earrings, ring-bearer's pillow, and flower girl's basket.

☐ Your veil can be borrowed from a close friend or sister who's recently been married. If you like the style and the shade matches your dress, why not? It can be your "something borrowed"—and it will save you money and time.

☐ The removable train from your veil can also make a lovely decoration, displayed at the reception hall. Displaying it will give guests a chance to admire the detail, and will look lovely near the cake and bridesmaids' bouquets.

☐ If you'll be dressing at the ceremony site, remember to check out the dressing room beforehand. Does it have a full-length mirror? Hangers? A sink? Take care of these things ahead of time (leave a few bottles of water if there's no sink), so you won't have to worry about them at the last minute.

☐ Remember to break in your wedding shoes well ahead of time—and remind your bridesmaids and any children in the wedding party to do the same. You don't want anyone falling, or even feeling shaky or slippery on their feet. You also don't want a flower girl to poop out before walking down the aisle, due to stiff shoes and aching feet!

☐ Bring comfortable dancing shoes to change into after the ceremony—you'll be glad you did.

☐ Have a "dress" rehearsal with everyone who'll be helping you dress on the day of the wedding, including how to attach and detach your train and veil. Don't assume the buttons, snaps, velcro, ties, and so on, will be simple to handle. And remember, you won't be able to see most of them.

☐ Give the members of your wedding party a photocopy of the processional and recessional plan (see the illustrations on pages 168 and 170). This will help avoid confusion, especially among attendants who are too embarrassed to admit at the rehearsal that they're not clear on where they should stand.

☐ Test new makeup, skin, and hair products in advance of the big day, to avoid allergic reactions and other unintended results. And remember to cover your face when putting on your wedding dress—you don't want makeup smudges. This applies to fittings as well as the wedding day.

☐ Ask the minister, priest, or rabbi to give you a copy of the wording of the ceremony in writing, so you can practice at home.

☐ If you're using candles in your ceremony, be careful! It's especially dangerous to use lighted candles as decorations in the church, at the end of each pew. Even your ceremonial candles should be handled with care, given your shaky nerves.

☐ Give the photographer a list of special guests you definitely want photos of. Don't leave it to chance; you won't find out until it's too late.

☐ Practice dancing with your fiancé. Many couples take dancing lessons before the wedding. At the very least, put on the song you'll be dancing to, and give it a whirl. (While you're at it, put on a few more songs, and give it a few more whirls. You don't want to feel awkward on the dance floor, when all eyes will be on you most of the night.)

☐ When planning the seating arrangements, put older guests far from the speakers. Opt for teenage and young-adult tables where the music will be loudest; they'll mind it the least, and they're likely to be on the dance floor anyway.

☐ In addition to giving the bandleader or DJ a list of songs you'd like played (including the songs for your first dance, your dance with your father, and the groom's dance with his mother, along with any other favorites), feel free to supply a list of songs you *don't* want played. Let them know if they can take requests from guests—and tell him exactly how much or how little you want him to talk. (Rent the movie *The Wedding Singer* if you need further convincing!)

☐ If the band has never played in this particular hall before, inform them of any special considerations, including any decorations that might interfere with the acoustics.

☐ Ask the bandleader or DJ to request that guests who've been married five, ten, twenty years, and so on, come to the dance floor to be honored for a dance.

☐ Confirm with the reception site that they will have sparkling, nonalcoholic cider or water for guests who do not drink. And make arrangements to take home unopened bottles of wine or champagne, if you've paid for them.

☐ If you're keeping your bouquet, ask the florist to create another, smaller one for you to toss.

☐ If you'd like to preserve the bridal bouquet, there are now ways to have it freeze-dried. This process keeps the beauty, shape, and color of the blooms. This must be prearranged. Visit the International Freeze-Dry Floral Association's home page at www.ifda.com.

☐ Another idea for personalizing your bridal bouquet is to have the florist create a miniature version that detaches from the main bouquet, to present to your mother when you reach the altar. This is a lovely tribute, and a nice surprise.

☐ Ask the photographer if he's worked at the wedding location before. What arrangements will he make in the event he falls ill on the big day. Is he prepared for foul weather? Don't be shy about calling to confirm that he knows the address and the time he should arrive.

☐ Consider hiring the photographer and videographer for a limited time rather than the full duration of the wedding. After the cake is cut and the first dance takes place, you might have all the pictures you need. Another way to cut video costs is to order the videotaping, but not the editing. You can edit the footage yourself (or leave it unedited) and save a lot of money.

☐ Try to use a bakery and florist you like and trust. (This goes for every service provider you use, but it's most applicable for the cake and flowers; not many of us hire bands or limousine drivers in our everyday lives!)

☐ It's become customary to supply toasting glasses and a cake cutter of your own. Before you purchase these items, ask close family members if they have any you could use. If you do purchase them, consider starting a family tradition by making the items available to future brides or grooms in the family.

☐ If you're announcing your engagement or wedding in the local newspaper, be sure not to list your home address. You don't want potential burglars to know where you live, and when you'll be out of the house.

☐ When sending your invitations, choose romantic or specially themed stamps; hearts, angels, botanical, and beach themes are all available. Remember, too, that oversized, odd-sized, and heavy invitations often require more than standard postage. Be sure to confirm the postage costs of your invitation and response card before ordering them (to avoid extra costs), and if you haven't, be sure to check this before mailing them out.

☐ If there are children in your wedding party, be sure there will be an adult stationed with them at the back of the church/ synagogue to calm jitters and get them ready to walk down the aisle.

☐ Pick out and purchase the bridesmaids' gifts early. Remember, they'll be handed out at the rehearsal dinner—but if you leave it until the last minute, you'll regret it, and you might have to settle for gifts that aren't perfect. Junior bridesmaids and flower girls should also be presented with a thank-you gift.

☐ To reduce stress among your bridesmaids, have drinks and light, unmessy snacks available before the ceremony. You won't be the only one who's nervous before the procession begins.

☐ Make seating cards yourself, to save money and add a handmade touch. This allows you to do them last minute, when all the final responses are in. Many couples put the cards in small picture frames, which serve as a small take-home gift for the guests (perfect for framing a photo of the wedding couple, if you include one with your thank-you notes).

☐ Prepare an emergency kit to take to the wedding and reception. Include safety pins, scissors, brush, comb, hairpins and hairspray, cottonballs, and an extra pair of pantyhose.

☐ Designate someone to collect your wedding gifts and other

personal belongings from the reception site. Make a list of items such as the toasting glasses, the top tier of the cake, cake topper and cake knife, guest books, leftover favors, ceremony candles, and so on, to make sure nothing is left behind. Bringing home flowers, to arrange around your gifts at home, is a lovely touch for the next day.

☐ Be sure to take pictures when opening your gifts. They make another nice keepsake, and you'll enjoy sharing them with the gift-givers, too.

☐ Don't forget to send postcards from your honeymoon—to both sets of parents and the others who made your day so special.

Special Tips from Recent Grooms

These suggestions come from former grooms across the country, so that you might benefit from their experience. While the tips and ideas throughout this planner apply to both the bride and the groom, this section is especially "for him."

- ☐ After you and your fiancée purchase your rings together, celebrate by taking her out to dinner. This is a milestone (and a big relief). Take a moment to enjoy it.
- ☐ Participate in the gift-registering process. It might seem like the bride's job, but it's something you should both have a hand in. After all, your relatives and friends will be selecting gifts off the list, too—and even more to the point, you'll be enjoying these items for years to come.
- ☐ While you're at a department store registering for gifts, consider shopping for some new luggage for your honeymoon. It's a nice way to treat yourself—and it will get you thinking about planning the big trip. Also pick up anything you know you'll need for the honeymoon—a new bathing suit, warm-weather clothing, etc.
- ☐ Make sure to double-check all your honeymoon reservations—hotels, planes, car service, etc., for the honeymoon. Don't let these important details get lost in the excitement of planning the wedding.
- ☐ If you're going abroad, make sure your passport is up to date.

Have traveler's checks ready, exchange currency in advance, and take care of any vaccinations and other requirements.

☐ Keep in mind that you should pick up the tab for the following flowers for the wedding: the bride's bouquet, the mothers' bouquets or corsages, and all boutonnieres (including the fathers'). Let the bride help in selecting these flowers (especially her bouquet), but you should pay for them.

☐ For the rehearsal of the wedding ceremony, request that the organist, any soloists, and the entire wedding party be present. Go over the entire service (minus your vows) a few times. Everyone should be clear on what they'll do when it's the real thing.

☐ Help your parents plan the rehearsal dinner. Remember, it's their responsibility. Remind them that the wedding party, plus spouses, are to be invited, and consult with them about who will likely be making a toast at the dinner. Talk to your father about the toast he'll make at the rehearsal dinner; tell him a toast you liked from another wedding you've attended.

☐ Prepare your own toast for the rehearsal dinner, thanking your parents for giving the dinner and also recognizing the bride's parents warmly.

☐ Request that your ushers have their measurements taken by a tailor, rather than an inexperienced friend or relative. Also, remind them to check all the pieces they've rented when they pick them up: Is everything there? Is everything the right size?

☐ Choose the gifts for your best man and ushers early. Favorites still include cuff links, pen and pencil sets, electronic organizers, picture frames, and nice wallets. Try to choose something they will keep and use for years to come. The gifts should be wrapped and presented at the rehearsal dinner. But don't leave it until the last minute!

☐ Request that your best man throw the bachelor party early—the week before the wedding. The night before the Big Day is not a good idea, since everyone (most of all you) will be tired and a little worse for wear.

☐ Start getting a little extra sleep two or three weeks before the wedding. You'll be glad you did.

- ☐ Practice uncorking a champagne bottle. It's unbecoming to send champagne stoppers flying across the room, or to let bubbly spill onto rugs or into your mouth—so practice. (It doesn't hurt to share a flute or two with your bride-to-be, while you're at it.)
- ☐ Make sure there will be ample parking for the guests, at both the church and the reception hall. If there isn't, make arrangements, and let your guests know where they should park.
- ☐ It's wise to put large umbrellas in the wedding party limos, in case of rain.
- ☐ The night before the wedding, remind the best man to put the rings in his tuxedo pocket, and check that you have your wedding license. It must be signed by the wedding official, with the best man and maid of honor as witnesses.
- ☐ At the altar, some groomsmen will be almost as nervous as you are (although they might not admit it!). They might chew gum to calm their nerves—which is not appropriate for the occasion. Very politely ask them to discard their gum before the ceremony begins.
- ☐ Practice de-stressing by slowing down your breathing, counting to five for each inhale and exhale. (The practice alone will calm you down, especially during those hectic days before the big day.) Just before you go to the altar, slow and steady breathing will keep you cool and collected. Are you nervous? No way!

INDEX

m 8076·C
9 元